creating
Messages
that connect

10 Secrets of Effective Communicators

alan **nelson**

Group

Loveland, Colorado
www.grouppublishing.com

Creating Messages That Connect: 10 Secrets of Effective Communicators
Copyright © 2004 Alan Nelson

Visit our Web site: **www.grouppublishing.com**

Credits
Senior Editor: Brian Proffit
Chief Creative Officer: Joani Schultz
Copy Editor: Lyndsay E. Gerwing
Art Director: Granite Design
Designer: Granite Design
Interior Illustrator: Dave Ridley
Print Production Artist: Granite Design
Cover Art Director/Designer: Jeff A. Storm
Production Manager: Peggy Naylor

Library of Congress Cataloging-in-Publication Data
Nelson, Alan E.
  Creating messages that connect : 10 secrets of effective communicators / by Alan Nelson.--1st American pbk. ed.
    p. cm.
Includes bibliographical references (p.   ).
ISBN 0-7644-2743-1 (pbk. : alk. paper)
1. Preaching. 2. Communication--Religious aspects--Christianity. I. Title.
BV4211.3.N45 2004
251--dc22

2004004343

10 9 8 7 6 5 4 3 2 1   13 12 11 10 09 08 07 06 05 04

Printed in the United States of America.

Dedication/Thanks

Dedicated to Katie, Courtney, and Kelsey Callahan and Jeff, Josh, and Jesse Nelson; six future, great communicators whom I love.

Thanks to "Pat," Dr. Patrick Marsh, who was a master professor at teaching about messages that work.

Thanks also to my friends and master communicators at Group Publishing—Brian Proffit, Paul Allen, Dave Thornton, Brad Lewis, Candace McMahan, Thom and Joani Schultz.

CONTENTS

A New Ministry Culture
Requires Learning a New Communication Style

BRIDGING THE GAP

While on a speaking trip to Guatemala, I sat in a hall filled with Central American pastors and church leaders who spoke Spanish. My español is pretty much limited to ordering from a Mexican restaurant menu, leftovers from my tres años of high school foreign language classes. Although the audience had translators when the English speakers taught, those of us unfamiliar with the native tongue were pretty much out of luck when indigenous teachers spoke. In spite of the excellence of their content and their energetic delivery, my mind wandered. While I'm sure they were committed to their messages, I felt bored. I did not understand what they were saying. It sounded like gibberish to me. I disconnected while they spoke, thinking about my lesson, wondering how my family was back home, and pondering the next meal's menu.

For pastors and church leaders to be effective as communicators today, we must learn to speak the native tongue. Postmodern, twenty-first–century (21C) America is a different culture from 20C.

If your call from God involves communicating, you're to be commended. Conveying the life-changing truth of God has never been in greater demand and has rarely been as difficult. The emphasis on quality, the competition of thousands of messages, and the stark realities of a changing culture make effective communication a challenge. Communicating is very difficult, even in optimum situations. Consider the large numbers of couples you know who speak the same language but can't communicate well.

Church attendance is declining. Ask the typical person on the street why he or she does not attend, and the top reason given is "It seems irrelevant and boring." Today most of us as pastors, in spite of good hearts and valiant attempts, do not speak the language of the land. We unintentionally bore our congregations with canned concepts, clichés, jargon, and monotonous monologue that sound like gibberish to today's crowd. The ageless truths of Scripture have not lost their power. New times require new strategies for connecting with those whom we serve.

Call it postmodernism, secularism, or whatever "ism" you like, society is changing. One result is that models of preaching developed in the twentieth century have lost much of their ability to connect with the twenty-first century. If it is true, as sociologists and church gurus tell us, that the culture in which we minister has dramatically morphed, then we'd better learn to speak 21C. We need to adopt new communication methods if we are to effectively convey the ageless truths of the Bible and Christ. Boring, de-motivating, and wandering sermons leave hungry parishioners with a sense of frustration.

While total church attendance is declining, the growing popularity of megachurch video cafes and satellite campuses implies that effective communicators are in higher demand than ever. The primary tool of the pastor is that of speaking/teaching. Surveys show that the greatest love of most pastors is their weekly message preparation and presentation. That means many of us are becoming less effective in the most important task of all that we do.

The time has come to not only sharpen the ax but also to consider a new ax head. Traditional preaching models have become outdated, gone the way of the 8-track, Pong video game, and typewriter. We all took homiletic and hermeneutic courses in Bible colleges and seminaries, but most of them fail to consider some of the most essential principles of communication. They pound the importance of "rightly dividing the word of truth," but they do little to deliver it hot and ready to eat for the famished listener. Understanding Greek and Hebrew, the context of the passage, and historical dynamics that made the Scripture powerful in its day are all valuable. But that understanding does not mean we understand the language of our day.

Relating to the culture of the day is not a complete cure either. We must become adept at bridge building, designing messages that connect

> *"We must preach with the Bible in one hand and the newspaper in the other."* (Karl Barth)

people with God. A message must be both delivered and received for it to be potentially effective. Reception of our messages has gone down significantly because we fail to translate them effectively. For some communicators it means picking up a different dialect. For others it means learning a whole new language. God's command to be good stewards demands that we take a serious look at the way we communicate the gospel.

MY STORY

I did not go to seminary to pursue a Master of Divinity. After a bachelor's in biblical literature, I wanted to learn how to communicate more effectively. In place of seminary, I pursued an interdisciplinary graduate degree in psychology and communication, with an emphasis on public speaking. If I was to invest the majority of my life communicating professionally, I wanted to better understand what made people tick and how I could design messages that they'd hear and from which they'd grow.

I was fortunate to sit under a very insightful professor, Dr. Patrick Marsh, who had authored a new textbook called *Messages That Work.*[1] Dr. Marsh created a very thorough model of communication that utilizes numerous matrices to describe elements of audience sophistication, complexity, information chunks, time, content density, and other aspects to understand why some messages work and others do not. Parts of this book are an application of this foundation to today's culture.

How will they know unless we tell them? You're a spokesperson for God. As a representative, it's your job to re-present him to people who've never known him or forgotten what he's like. Because God created people and then sent his Son to die for them, we'd better learn how to most effectively communicate the good news. We can't focus our sole communicative efforts on understanding the Word of God, systematic theology, hermeneutics, and homiletics and hope to do our job in connecting with people. We must learn to design messages that engage attention, are structured to make sense, answer perceived needs, raise the awareness of unknown needs, and flow toward a specific goal. The weekly feeding of the flock is the most critical single moment in the life of the local congregation. Raising the bar in this area is possible for nearly all of us. The result is greater connection with our listeners and, as a result, more fulfillment. You can learn to hone your message preparation skills so that people will walk away with increased excitement, retention, and spiritual truth.

DESIGN PRINCIPLES THAT WORK

Every day advertisers and political speechwriters invest large amounts of money and energy into designing specific messages for maximum impact. If Procter & Gamble, Nike, and Budweiser take the time and effort to invest millions of dollars into messages that sell soap, shoes, and beer, we should take our message preparation seriously. Souls are at stake. Eternities are in the balance. We're called to unpack the most powerful, life-changing message in history to people who desperately need it in these confusing times. Because communication is more art than science, there will always be fuzziness and unknowns. Effective message design will not automatically turn you into a John Ortberg, Rick Warren, Josh McDowell, Andy Stanley, or T.D. Jakes, but it will improve your preaching and teaching. Your messages can connect with people. Your messages *must* connect with people. The kingdom needs them to do that.

Good communicators are those who develop an effective style for a specific group of people. *Great* communicators are able to adapt their presentation to a variety of groups so that in any given setting, their style, form, and content may differ significantly from the previous message. These principles, used by great communicators, can help you connect with your listeners more powerfully, even if you communicate only with a fairly narrow range of people.

How would you like to improve your ability to communicate? You *can* be more effective. What are

> *Communicating the gospel is far too important for us to merely rely on our knowledge of the Bible with a couple of illustrations added to the mix. We must learn to connect with our hearers.*

Don't put prepara-tion instructions on your spiritual food packaging, assum-ing people will go home and pop it in the oven. Think in terms of preparing your message like a ready-to-eat meal.

the keys that set excellent communicators above average ones? The goal of this book is for you to develop your unique style, in a way that makes you more effective. Good communicators come in a wide variety of forms. Some are smooth and articu-late. Others are funny and animated. Some are stoic and profound. Yet others are casual and even rough-sounding. But they all have one thing in common: They connect with their listeners. Our objective is not fewer "ums" or more vocal resonance. We want people to "get it" after we've finished. This isn't about public speaking. It's about communicating. A dozen smooth-tongued orators aren't worth a single communicator who connects. The latter is what we're about because as men and women of the Message, our responsibility is great.

The gospel is not irrelevant, boring, or impotent. It has never been more exciting, interesting, and effective for life transformation than today. The problem, more often than not, is in how it is communicated. Our goal is to raise the level of fruitfulness of your preaching, teaching, and speaking so that God's work is expanded.

COMING TO TERMS WITH TERMS

We pastors are a funny lot. We come in a broad variety of shapes and sizes, traditions and preferences, but there's something about us that you can usually smell a mile away. Some may think it a celestial aura or a holy aroma. Spend time around even the most contemporary of us, and you get a whiff of *Eau de Ecclesia*. Opinions on theology and ministry are legion, diverse, and robust. That's why some of us may already feel offended to read about an audience instead of a congregation, preach-ing with a newspaper in one hand (symbolically of course), or even sug-gesting that typical seminary training is insufficient to grasp the gist of effective communicating. Please grant me latitude as we discuss com-munication principles.

For the sake of practicing what I preach, let's define some terms that we'll use in the rest of this book. We'll periodically use the word *sender* to represent a person who is giving a message, since not all messages are given via speaking. We'll sometimes use the term *receiver* to refer to a person who is intended to capture the message, since *listener* implies a spoken word. *Audience* can refer to a small or large group in a Sunday school class, home Bible study, or congregation. This makes it easier than hopscotching around terms such as parishioners, congregants, hearers, and so on. *Message design* is generic, pertaining to any type of communication preparation. To most of us, it means a weekend sermon or Bible lesson. That is why we'll typically illustrate in the context of weekly pastoral speaking responsibilities.

Sometimes it's easy to tell who slept through the service.

Section 1
The Ten Secrets

Chapter One
Secret #1

Answer the Question
"Why Should I Listen to You?"

WHY SHOULD JOHN AND SARAH LISTEN?

L ast week John put in a sixty-hour workweek, which included two days on the road, one overnight in a hotel, and making connections with four planes in the process. The other three days in town were overflowing with staff meetings, conference calls among existing and potential customers, and a couple of late nights strategizing about right-sizing the company. Open evenings and the weekend were invested in paying bills, taking care of household duties, helping the kids with homework, and trying to hit the gym. John's the assistant coach of his son's soccer team, and his daughter is taking dance, making John and his wife, Sarah, a busy couple. Although he was raised in the church, John checked out as soon as he began college. Church just didn't seem to be his thing. Now, with a family and sensing a need for moral teaching and spiritual guidance, John and Sarah have returned to church.

Today Pastor Jeff Smyth begins a new series out of the book of Isaiah. He starts in chapter 1, discussing Isaiah's warning to the rebellious nation. He provides some interesting biographical material on the prophet, as well as historical information about Israel, before explaining the main points of the warning. While there's nothing wrong with the presentation, John is having a difficult time concentrating. His mind keeps going over the issues he's struggling with at work. An occasional nudge from Sarah reminds him to get back to listening to the message, but nothing seems to grab him. These things happened so many years ago.

After the service, John and Sarah shake hands with the pastor and say, "Thank you, Pastor Jeff. We've never studied Isaiah. That was interesting." They walk to their car and drive home without any conversation on the results of Pastor Jeff's ten to fifteen hours of message preparation. The sermon seemed so foreign to the world in which they live. If it was up to John, he'd probably pass on attending church, but for the sake of Sarah and the kids, he tries to do his best to show up when they can fit it into their weekend schedule. John and Sarah have considered trying another church, but the half-dozen they visited prior to Faith Fellowship seemed pretty much the same. Since their kids were happy and it was within a few minutes of their house, they decided to end their search; after all, it was the church they disliked the least.

John and Sarah are typical of church attendees today. While they aren't thrilled with what they've found, they attend out of a sense of duty and responsibility because it seems the right thing to do.

Remember when you were a kid and you wanted a snack before dinner?

"Mom, can I have a treat?"

"No," she said.

"Why?" you asked.

"Because I said so," she responded.

We hated that response then, and we'd likely reject it now if our supervisor gave us such a weak response. But many pastors answer their congregants as our mothers did. When parishioners subliminally ask, "Why should I listen to you?" we silently respond with the equivalent of...

"It's good for you."

"God would want it that way."

"I'm professionally trained to represent our Lord."

"We've always done it this way."

"Because I said so."

"I'm busy. Life is short. So please make it clear why I should invest one to two hours of my life here at church."

Guilt, tradition, a love for God, or other ministry offerings compel many people to keep attending *in spite of,* not because of, the Sunday morning message. It's not that a majority of these messages are totally void of biblical truth and helpful content. The problem is that these things tend to get lost in jargon, muddy main points, disjointed thought progression, and an antiquated presentation style. Retro preaching is not in vogue as some might think. Sadly, most Johns and Sarahs have given up hope of finding relevant help within Sunday morning messages. They assume that boring, religious-sounding sermons are a part of the typical church experience.

Every weekend well over 300,000 sermons are preached in America.[1] Worship services continue to be the single most highly attended event at any one time in spite of the popularity of media and sports. Most consider the sermon to be the summit of this event. Each weekend, the church has one grand opportunity to either buck the trend of declining interest in Christianity or reinforce the growing percentage of religious skeptics. After listening to the one-third million messages preached, most hearers, if asked to be really honest, would admit that they were less than satisfied. Many sincere Christians have drawn the conclusion that it's not truly a good sermon unless they've been bored, clichéd, or raked over the coals. Others leap to the assumption that if a message even appears to be engaging or entertaining, then the minister must be watering down the gospel in order to tickle ears. We've justified mediocre preaching as a qualification for biblical truth, confusing presentation with content. An entertaining, biblical sermon is considered an oxymoron.

WHAT MAKES TODAY'S CROWD TOUGH

Stand-up comedians say an audience is tough when it doesn't laugh at their humor. A ten-minute routine can feel like eternity when people aren't responding. "Help me; I'm dying up here," the comedian says to himself. "You're killing us," the audience declares in silence. Today's church and would-be church audiences are tougher crowds than in the past. Preaching styles, which have changed little since the '50s and '60s,

16

are killing today's congregants. Here are seven reasons today's audiences are so easily bored with what we have to say and/or the way we say it.

1. They're conditioned by fast living and media. Funny, we used to think modern technology would give us more time to relax. In many ways, it has done the opposite, increasing the pace of living. In-your-face advertising, thirty-second commercials interrupting programs every eight to twelve minutes, and sound/sight bites have shortened our attention spans. A news event that's considered especially important will receive up to three minutes on the national news, while most get only forty-five or even five seconds. In the '90s, we began to see television sitcoms and dramas such as *Friends, Seinfeld, The Practice,* and *Law & Order* change style, cutting quickly from scene to scene and story line to story line. Viewers want story lines to keep moving. Just like replacing a video projector with an overhead projector, slow-motion messages make us feel like we've gone back in history.

2. They're spoiled by multiple options. The standing joke about men and their remote controls is that women are interested in what's on TV, whereas men are interested in what *else* is on TV. When we have over one hundred options on cable or the satellite dish, not to mention countless brands of deodorant and who knows how many food varieties at our disposal, getting the same ol', same ol' at church just doesn't cut it. The vanilla style with which most of us approach preaching seems overly tame to the consummate consumer. People are pickier than they've ever been. Excellence sells, even in communication, so people are apt to pick communicators they like best.

3. They're used to immediate gratification and instant information. The power of the Internet has made all of us less tolerant of slowness. Bored with a Web site? Download taking too long? Click,

> *"Preachers address an audience that comes to church with clickers in their heads. In modern culture, people distinguish quickly between the interesting and the tedious. They scan the newspaper for stories that catch their minds. They flip through magazines and read the first sentence or the opening paragraph to decide whether it 'sounds interesting.' They vote in the first thirty seconds whether to tune in or turn off the channel."*
>
> —MARK GALLI AND CRAIG BRIAN LARSON[2]

we're off to something else. Instant messaging, cell phones, real-time communication, and Internet shopping have conditioned us to feel, if not think, that we should have access to information right away and in a format that fits our preference. Computer/Internet/cell technologies are equivalent to the second Gutenberg press in impact, completely transforming how we do life.

4. They're used to multi-tasking. We drive to work while sipping a Starbucks coffee and talking on the phone. We help the kids with their homework as we fold clothes and watch TV. We catch breaking news on CNN while reading the scrolling ticker tape and weather report at the bottom of the screen. Although we can sit around and discuss the theoretical benefits of solemnity, solitude, and slowing down, the bottom line is that it's getting more difficult for people to do only one thing at a time. When they try, they feel that life is passing them by. When they come to church to watch the equivalent of a talking head lecture for twenty to forty minutes or more, it's probably one of the most adrenaline-deprived moments of their week. Mind-wandering, fidgeting, grogginess, and feelings of under-stimulation run rampant in today's church audiences. Good manners and holy fear keep most from admitting their boredom, but mono-tasking seems archaic.

5. They've experienced top-drawer communicators. That's right, the best speakers have let the cat out of the bag: The Bible can be interesting and understood. People can hear effective female and male communicators at conferences, on television and radio, and via DVD-video and CD-Rom. People who move into the 'hood after attending ABC megachurch with Rev. XYZ super speaker now stare at most of us with a glint of disappointment. A growing number in our audiences are like the old boy who turned to his wife in curlers and a housecoat after watching a Miss America pageant and said, "Well, I suppose you'll do." Failing to measure up to excellent communicators is a growing issue, leaving people less satisfied with poor preaching than ever before.

6. They're more secular and less motivated to learn. Pastors of committed Christians have an advantage over those in seeker-oriented congregations. Christians tend to be more motivated to learn the Bible, more willing to work at understanding and applying ageless truths. Secular crowds not only don't believe absolute truth exists, but they've often not yet bought into the concept that Jesus has a better idea. Depending on what studies you read, the United States is between the third and sixth most non-Christian nation in the world. Sitting around with committed Christians, complaining "this isn't right" does not change the reality in which we live. We cannot assume a basic Christian orientation.

> *"Your greatest competition is not your competition. It is indifference."*
> —HARRY BECKWITH[3]

7. They're change-oriented. Many people who attend church on cultural holidays, such as Christmas and Easter, don't come back because they feel like nothing has changed. Nearly everything in other realms of life is upgrading, improving, and evolving. We're suspicious of things that seem to stay the same. Contemporary thinking has little patience for systems and styles perceived as archaic. Society tends to stamp the word *dinosaur* on anything that seems old-fashioned and resistant to change.

So what should we do? Add some pyrotechnics to our services? Forgo our typical worship for vaudeville? Should we provide IV adrenaline drip lines for each seat? Employ dancing girls and a halftime show?

Starting to feel depressed by what you're up against? What's the use? Let's just plug in a DVD of a popular communicator and take a seat among our listeners.

Times are tough for effective communicating in the church. The challenges we face can either intimidate us to quit trying or motivate us to get better. William Bridges said leaders invest too much effort into selling solutions; we should sell the problem first.[4] Understanding what we're up against as effective Christian communicators in 21C should provide a wake-up call. Many of us think we're doing better than we are. While these seven factors affect more than just the first secret of effective communicating, they definitely impact the initial question: "Why should I listen to you?"

CAN YOU SAY, *"RELEVANT"*?

Awhile ago, I heard a nationally recognized pastor, author, and seminary president speak at a gathering. He said, "One of the words I hate

> *"We don't see things as they are, we see them as we are."*
>
> -ANAÏS NIN [5]

the most is *relevant.*" He went on to explain why he thought the drive to be relevant was prostituting modern preaching, reducing it to a spiritually impotent practice. Although he and I are in the same business, our ideologies are quite different. That leader's audience is highly Christianized, while mine is much broader. We believe in the same objectives but quite different methodologies. The primary reason for ineffective pulpit work is failing to show our listeners why the message matters in their lives. According to R.C. Sproul, "To say that theology is boring is really to say that God is boring. And yet, part of the problem is that the average person in the pew is not likely to get a steady diet of theology that is proclaimed with excitement and relevance."[6]

John Stott, a well-respected English preacher, described a conversation that changed the way he approached communicating. He was talking with the two sons of a Christian couple. One son had become an atheist and the other an agnostic.

"What had happened? I asked. Was it that they no longer believed Christianity to be true? 'No', they replied, 'that's not our problem. We're not really interested to know whether Christianity is true...What we want to know...is not whether Christianity is *true*, but whether it's *relevant.* And frankly we don't see how it can be...What possible relevance can a primitive Palestinian religion have for us?' "[7]

The word *relevant* means "bearing upon or connected with the matter at hand; pertinent; having practical value or applicability." Messages that connect are relevant by their very essence. They bring to light scriptural truths that are of practical value and are applicable to everyday life. Relevant messages lift up truth that is pertinent to the receiver. Irrelevant messages may be packed with truth, but they fail to connect with the receivers in terms of benefits. The greatest preaching sin of today is failing to make messages relevant. As stewards of God's Word, it is our responsibility to help people understand the pertinence of a truth. We must connect kingdom principles to everyday living in such a way that people say, "Oh, I see. I need that."

There are undoubtedly risks in making relevance the driving motivation behind preaching. When we allow people to set the agenda of

what we preach or how we teach, we tend to wander from the truth. Situationalism suggests that
truth varies from situation to situation, so we fail to
find an anchor in the Bible, which is enduring and
foundational. A focus on relevance can lead pastors down the road of relying on pop psychology,
folklore, news events, and philosophizing in the

> *The single most
> important motivator
> for adult learners is
> "Does this address a
> problem I perceive?"*

pulps. Sharing your thoughts on how people should live is often void of
biblical truth. Overemphasizing relevance can also end up making the
biblical text fit what you want to say. The result is distorted context and
sermons that are little more than humanistic talks.

While we cannot ignore these risks in pursuing relevance without
boundaries, we dare not overlook the dangers of ignoring relevance.
When we fail to make clear the relevance of our topic, people check out,
negating our efforts. They assume that if there's nothing there that can
help them, then there's little need for them to listen. When we fail to
help people understand the relevance of the passage we're unpacking,
we reinforce the natural inclination to segregate religion from our everyday lives. This disengagement creates shallow Christians who exude
church behavior and attitudes while at church but fail to live them out
in their businesses, marriages, relationships, priorities, attitudes, and
stewardship. The world is full of people whose knowledge of the Bible
far exceeds their application of its truths. A danger of not making our
messages relevant is that we give people great Bible content without giving them the handles of knowing how to pick it up and use it.

The parable of the sower (Luke 8:5ff) refers to God's Word as seeds.
Some fall on a hardened path, and the birds eat it. Others drop among
the rocks and die for lack of moisture. Another lies among weeds and is
overgrown by them. The final lands on good soil and produces a great
crop. While the story is brief and primarily a metaphor for why people
respond to the gospel the way they do, every farmer knows that you
don't just fling seeds if you want them to grow. You have to prepare the
soil to receive the seeds.

Much of my father's life during the spring of each year was invested
in plowing, disking, harrowing, and fertilizing so that when he planted,
the seeds would grow. Message design is equivalent to preparing the soil

prior to planting the seeds. Our job is not to merely fling God's Word to our audiences each week. We must do it in such a way that it is most apt to have a chance to take root and grow.

ADULT LEARNING

The University of Phoenix is headquartered in the metropolitan area where I live. With more than 125,000 students across 117 campuses and the Internet, it is one of the largest national distributors of collegiate education in the nation.[8] UoP is distinguished from more traditional universities in that its primary clientele are adult students, rather than people in their late teens and early twenties. The methods the school uses match the needs and learning styles of adult learners. Most of the courses are taught not by professional academicians but by degreed practitioners. The main reason for this is that, as they teach the course content, they illustrate it with real-world examples and explain how the principles work in everyday life.

"I want to learn. I want to like it. I really do. But I'm tired, so please don't make me work for the reason to listen to this message."

A significant psychological difference between adult learners and others is that *adults want to know that what they're learning applies to the real world and, even more important, answers a problem they're confronting.* Adults are not interested in solutions for which they do not perceive problems. They're too busy and experienced to waste time on information that has little relevance. They want truth that connects with their everyday lives. If it does not or if it is not clear, then adults tend to tune out. That's why it is so important that you answer the unspoken question at the beginning of your talk: "Why should I listen to you?" They want to know how it will benefit their marriages, get them closer to God, solve a question they've always pondered, clarify their decision-making process, or any of a thousand possibilities that legitimately can be taught through the Bible.

Haddon Robinson says, "Sermons catch fire when flint strikes steel. When the flint of a person's problem strikes the steel of the Word of God, a spark ignites that burns in the mind. Directing our preaching at people's needs is not a mere persuasive technique; it is the task of the ministry."[9]

If the Bible is the source of all we need to know to live the kind of life God desires, then we should not fear connecting it to people's lives. Pastors who downplay relevance or fear focusing on felt needs are neglecting their duty. I've heard traditionalists critically quote Isaiah 55:8-11:

> "For my thoughts are not your thoughts, neither are your ways my ways," declares the Lord. "As the heavens are higher than the earth, so are my ways higher than your ways and my thoughts than your thoughts. As the rain and the snow come down from heaven, and do not return to it without watering the earth and making it bud and flourish, so that it yields seed for the sower and bread for the eater, *so is my word that goes out from my mouth: It will not return to me empty,* but will accomplish what I desire and achieve the purpose for which I sent it" (emphasis added).

These traditionalists interpret it like this: "God's Word will not return void. All we have to do is preach the Word, and it will do its job. Our responsibility is not to heighten the attractiveness of Scripture, add illustrations to it, or strive to make it relevant." But the context of this passage refers to God speaking, not preachers or prophets. Since we're not God, we should not hope that merely reading God's Word to others will naturally produce results. Even if we suggest that this passage is not limited to God speaking, we still cannot claim that we have only limited responsibility to help people understand the Word and clarify its relevance to them. Jesus did not merely quote Scriptures, assuming people would make the connection. He constantly used word pictures, explained meanings, and spoke in terms that, for the most part, his audiences could understand.

"Do your best to present yourself to God as one approved, a workman who does not need to be ashamed and who correctly handles the word of truth" (2 Timothy 2:15).

If your theological bias is to disregard the importance of relevance, the purpose of this book is not to dissuade you. Preachers who are gifted speakers can likely find a supportive audience, interested only in understanding the Scriptures, regardless of relevance or practical application. But this crowd is quickly shrinking in the twenty-first century. Our conviction is that correctly handling the Word of truth requires that we translate it into everyday contexts so that receivers can more easily distill what

> *"Good communication is stimulating as black coffee, and just as hard to sleep after."*
> —ANNE MORROW LINDBERGH[10]

the gospel looks like, incarnate in twenty-first–century subcultures. Most believers consume Bible knowledge without putting it into practice, in part because pastors fail to help them make a connection. We cannot think we've fulfilled our responsibility once we've delivered the groceries, assuming they'll prepare the meal on their own. Today we have to present spiritual food hot, ready to eat, and even aesthetically appealing.

The solution is to begin and end your message preparation with this reality check: Feel your sermon from the perspective of the people in the seats. They are asking, "Why should I invest the next twenty to forty minutes of my life listening to you? Why is this important? How is it going to change my life? Why is it crucial that I pay attention? Why will I not want to miss what you're about to say? How will my life not be as good if I do not grasp what you're about to tell me?"

One way of accomplishing this is to do some of your message preparation outside of your study. Go to a coffeehouse or shopping mall, and work on your preparation from a laptop or notepad. Look at the people around you, and imagine what they would say about your message. How do you think it could be said in such a way that it would help the common passersby? How would you communicate it in such a way that they would not stare at you with glossy eyes or, worse, mutter to themselves, "Baloney!" This practice helps you stay honest with yourself.

Those of us on the professional side of ministry already buy into the truth of the Bible and the tenets of Christianity. Most of the people "out there" don't. Even those in our church who've bought into the basics live and work among masses who doubt, and their skepticism rubs off on them. Assume your people are saying, "Yeah, sure; prove it." Don't assume they can apply your message to their everyday lives. Presume they need to know immediately why it's important to them. They will decide at the beginning of your talk whether to listen or check out. A relevancy statement or question lets the potential listener know what he or she can expect to receive from the message.

WHY SHOULD PEOPLE LISTEN TO YOU?

A relevancy statement can ask a provocative or rhetorical question, promise a felt-need solution, or introduce the theme in some other way that causes receivers to desire to listen.

Here are three examples of opening relevancy statements that seek to answer the question "Why should I listen to you?" These are not suggested as actual message openings, but they do define the relevance of a text. Relevancy statements are more straightforward for topical messages, so I'll give examples for expository messages. These would change, depending on the audience and your awareness of its perceived needs.

1. Text: 1 Corinthians 13 (characteristics of God's love combined with the truth that God is love). A lot of us claim to have God in our lives. But have you ever wanted evidence that God is in your life? Today we're going to look at thirteen symptoms that help demonstrate whether God is in you or not. (Proceed with the passage that God is love, 1 John 4:16, and follow by unpacking 1 Corinthians 13:4-8.)

2. Text: Jonah 2 (Jonah's prayer in the belly of the fish). Have you ever been so low that you felt like calling it quits, giving up, raising the white flag? What kind of prayer do you pray when you pretty much feel that all hope is gone? Today we are going to look at a powerful prayer, given by a man who was down for the count. (Unpack the prayer of surrender by Jonah as he was preparing for his death.)

3. Text: Philemon (the return of his slave, Onesimus, after becoming a believer). Have you ever wondered what it means to have authentic faith? Have you questioned why it seems so many people are hypocritical, living everyday lives

> *"American business may have discovered the value of clarity. In a National Association of Colleges and Employers survey of 480 companies and public organizations, the quality most sought by employers was not motivation, which ranked third, or academic credentials and performance, which ranked sixth. It was the ability to communicate."[11]*

that are quite different from their church lives? Today we're going to look at a person whose inside matched his outside and how we can increase our integrity. (Unpack the story of Onesimus' faith and integrity compelling him to do the right thing by returning to his owner, Philemon, in spite of the risk of being punished.)

Graham Johnston said, "A fallout of the consumer age is people have grown cynical of always being targeted for a sale, and this cynicism extends to the church. Postmodern people view their time as a commodity, and a precious one, so the very thought of 'wasting' a Sunday morning with little or no take-home value is repugnant." [12]

Sometimes you can actually see it go right over their heads.

Dennis Fletcher, 17 Ruth Dr., Monroe City, MO 63456, dfletch76@socket.net. Used by artist's permission. Reprinted from Leadership Journal.

Discussion/Thought Prompters

1. What's your view on balancing understanding the Bible in its true essence with the need to focus on relevance for the audience?
2. What do you think makes communicating today such a challenge?
3. Think of a communicator you thoroughly enjoy. What are some of the attributes that make him or her effective? What does this tell you about his or her skills? What does this reveal about your perceived needs/interests?
4. What are two or three things you'd like to improve in your communicating?
5. What can you do this week to raise the perception of relevance in this Sunday's message? (Try writing a couple of viable relevancy statements.)

Chapter Two

Secret #2

Know Your Audience

PREACHING VERSUS COMMUNICATING

What is the difference between a typical preacher/Bible teacher and a communicator? A preacher/teacher starts with the message. He strives to present a passage or biblical theme in a way as similar as possible to the original biblical text. A communicator starts with the audience. He attempts to understand receivers in order to know how best to present the message. While these distinctions may be artificial and even exaggerated, it helps us see how the two types of message senders go about their goal differently. Theologians, not communication specialists, staff most college religion departments and seminaries. They go to great effort to explain contextual details, translation issues, and other homiletic matters. All of these are vital, but they are usually not sufficient.

To suggest that the audience comes first sounds heretical to some, akin to rubbing the cat the wrong way. "How can you say that the message does not come first? How can you expect to communicate if you do not know how to 'rightly divide the word of truth'?" But saying that communicators first strive to understand the audience does not mean they take the message lightly. Communicators realize that no matter how well they use study helps and scriptural tools, the results are no better than casting pearls to swine if they fail to connect with the receivers.

> **Just a thought:**
> *Preachers care about the gospel. Communicators care about people. The gospel is that Jesus died for* people *because he loves them.*

Perhaps that is why Jesus had so many different ways of communicating kingdom principles. He used a myriad of word pictures and parables because he understood the needs of his audiences. He could have used theological jargon but insisted on speaking in terms of shepherds, vineyards, water, sparrows, unjust judges, good Samaritans, and fig trees. His stories changed according to his audiences, while the truths remained consistent. The issue is not a matter of either knowing the audience or Scriptures but knowing *both* the audience and Scriptures. Preaching is about forth-telling, transmitting truths. Communicating is about the sender and receiver literally "coming together."

The difficulty for most of us preachers lies in knowing the audience. Mark Galli and Craig Brian Larson wrote, "We're more interested in the subject than in the people. The first act of love in preaching is an act of self-denial...giving up the love of knowledge and replacing it with a love for people...A good editor edits by a simple but effective motto: The reader first. Preachers would do well to preach by a similar motto: Hearers first."[1]

Churches attracting the unchurched are often accused of watering down the gospel. Certainly, this should be a concern in any church. But for most of us in congregations attracting God-explorers, the issue is not a matter of watering down the message but of making sure people don't choke on it. If we overwhelm them with terminology, concepts, and heady exegesis they do not understand, we risk numbing them to the good news. The use of visual aids, movie clips, PowerPoint, drama, and other multimedia are simply modern means of storytelling. Good communicators are good storytellers. The best communicators use word pictures to which their audiences will relate. Preaching guru Haddon Robinson said, "The age of the preacher is gone, the age of the communicator has arrived."[2]

MISSIONAL THINKING

Communicators are like missionaries in their thinking. They get to know the culture, language, values, artifacts, customs, and religious ideas of those with whom they hope to communicate. Christian sociologists and culture analysts recognize that most post-2000 audiences think differently from those in the preceding century. The percentage of our listeners who understand evangelical terminology and Christian-ese is shrinking. Our three options are much the same as missionaries face:

1. We can miscommunicate by sticking to older forms of message sending.

2. We can employ translators who are able to take what we say and put it into language understood by indigenous people.

3. We can learn the ways and customs of postmodern locals, along with message design principles, in order to communicate in ways they will hear and understand.

Jesus was missional. He was a communicator. Through the Incarnation, he became like one of us.

Paul's communication philosophy in 1 Corinthians 9:19-27 is an ageless treatise on missional thinking (non-italics text is my extrapolation):

"Though I am free and belong to no man, I make myself a slave to everyone, to win as many as possible." I am willing to give up my preferred way of being heard; I am willing to work to change, in order to help others know about God and hopefully find the good news of Christ.

"To the Jews I became like a Jew, to win the Jews. To those under the law I became like one under the law (though I myself am not under the law), so as to win those under the law. To those not having the law I became like one not having the law (though I am not free from God's law but am under Christ's law), so as to win those not having the law. To the weak I became weak, to win the weak. I have become all things to all men so that by all possible means I might save some. I do all this for the sake of the gospel, that I may share in its blessings." If I am to be effective at connecting with people (which is the essence of communication and essential to presenting the gospel), I realize it is not about me, but about them—understanding my receivers. I will make every effort to learn their ways for the purpose of communicating God's

life-transforming news. I'm motivated to fulfill the Great Commission and experience the fruit of that pursuit.

"Do you not know that in a race all the runners run, but only one gets the prize? Run in such a way as to get the prize. Everyone who competes in the games goes into strict training. They do it to get a crown that will not last; but we do it to get a crown that will last forever. Therefore I do not run like a man running aimlessly; I do not fight like a man beating the air. No, I beat my body and make it my slave so that after I have preached to others, I myself will not be disqualified for the prize." I can't just assume people want to hear my words or will understand what I have to say. No, I take very seriously the complex process of communication, and I will relentlessly hone my skills at designing messages that hit the target. I refuse to take the easy way and rely on past training or familiar methods. I will discipline myself to constantly learn new ways of presenting ageless truths so that I can provide people with a legitimate understanding of the gospel and kingdom living.

Haddon Robinson wrote, "The most important single factor in whether or not you are an effective communicator lies in whether or not you doggedly [ask]…'Who are my listeners?'…We don't teach the Bible. We teach *people* the Bible. As vital as it is to know content, it's not enough. We must know our audiences."[4]

Communication doesn't just happen. Messages that connect are intentional, designed, and carefully presented.

FIVE AUDIENCE FACTORS

There are five primary audience-analysis factors that significantly influence effective message design.

1. Demographics (age, education, gender, culture, socioeconomic level): These are basic blueprint issues that significantly affect a person's communication filters.

Age: How old are your targeted receivers? While generational differences are at times exaggerated, they do affect how people think, receive, and process messages. Bridgers, busters, boomers, and builders represent varying stages of life, with correspondingly varying views. But remember that the differences are based more on current age than on generation. When you study a group of busters during their twenties, you're going to get information indicative of people in their twenties. Their views will change as they move through their thirties, forties, and fifties.

Education: The level of formal education and training in your audience is also important. As you address people with higher education, you'll generally want to increase message density and complexity and use more specialized terminology. (We'll explain these concepts later.) The lower the average education of the audience, the more you'll need to simplify ideas, stick to everyday language, and use less complex illustrations.

Gender: Is the audience male, female, or mixed? Women's groups respond quite differently from men's groups, and mixed groups differ as well. Men tend to prefer sticking with left-brain functions, while women tend toward using the right hemisphere or both. This affects the way your receivers process input.

Culture: Both national and local ethnicities shape values, language, style, and tastes. Is the audience from the Midwest, South, East, Southwest, or other? Are they rural, urban, or suburban? Are they Anglo, Hispanic, African-American, or Asian? The more you know about distinct groups in your audience, the better your chances at designing messages that hit the target. We've all experienced outside speakers who obviously were out of touch with local norms and customs.

Socioeconomic level: What is the mean income of the receivers? Affluent audiences perceive different needs in their lives from those with middle and lower incomes. People's money stream often affects their motives, spiritual responsiveness, and felt needs.

2. Readiness: A person's readiness is primarily motivational: "How ready am I to receive the message? Am I anticipating it, neutral, or wishing I wasn't here?"

Motivation usually requires a certain level of information. Often a lack of response is due more to ignorance than resistance. For example, when Jesus spoke to the woman at the well, he did not find a resistant audience. She merely needed to be informed about the possibility of living water. That was all it took to get her excited about hearing more.

Many of our listeners aren't really resistant to the Bible and Christianity; they just lack vital information about them. Most people do not reject God as much as their perceptions about him—which are usually based on a concoction of hearsay, personal experiences, toxic theology, and non-credible demonstrations of faith. It is not our responsibility to spin the gospel to make it more palatable. The gospel can stand up for itself, by itself. Our job is to figure out the best means and manner to connect with our hearers so what they get is the true good news and not some version adulterated by traditions, personal bias, bad experience, and incompetent communication means. Authentic, clearly communicated gospel messages generally find a receptive ear in our spiritually intrigued culture. When nonbelievers reject Christianity, most assume it is the message they do not accept, but often the problem was the manner in which the message was communicated. Never assume a person is rejecting a message until you know for certain he or she is not rejecting the manner, medium, or messenger.

Readiness asks the question "How motivated is my audience to listen and learn?" When you are working with people who have low readiness, you are going to have to initially invest more of your time engaging them, giving them a reason for receiving your communication. You need to take extra care not to bore or overwhelm them. When you fail to hold people's attention, you'll lose them and, thus, fail to communicate. In other words, there is a greater need to sell them on how they can benefit from what you're about to say.

One method for holding their attention is entertainment. Telling jokes or an interesting story or showing an appropriate video clip or drama will help engage your listeners' attention so you can increase their level of readiness. Some speakers miss the mark by failing to connect the entertainment to the topic at hand. Entertainment for entertainment's sake is usually insufficient, although an exception can be made when a communicator is unknown and humor or stories are used to break the ice, endearing the audience to the speaker. In general, though, we need to make sure the entertainment leads logically to the message.

"Augustine...defined the preacher's task as docere, deletare, flectere—*to teach, to delight, to influence. To touch the mind, the heart, the will."*[5]

In church, we frequently overestimate our listeners' readiness to learn and apply the principles we are about to share, and we fail to develop a motivational climate at the beginning of the message. But conversely, when you have a ready audience, don't

> *"Give a bonus to leaders who do a good job, especially the ones who work hard at preaching and teaching"* (1 TIMOTHY 5:17, THE MESSAGE).

waste time selling them on the message. They will become frustrated and often tune out if you do not get on with the message.

Our depth of information must match our listeners' readiness. We've all had experiences when we've asked someone, "How are you doing?" and she's proceeded to spend the next half hour giving us the details of her week. She overestimated our readiness to listen. Conversely, most of us guys have had numerous times our wives were quite ready to hear every detail of our day, and we responded with the USA Today summary.

It can happen to preachers, too, as illustrated in this well-worn story: The farmer was the only one who made it to church during a Sunday morning blizzard. The preacher asked him, "Do you want me to preach my sermon or not?" The farmer replied, "If I only had one cow that showed up to eat, I'd feed her." The preacher launched into a forty-five–minute monologue. When finished, he asked the quiet farmer, "So what do you think?" The farmer said, "If I had one cow that showed up to eat, I'd feed her...but I wouldn't dump the whole load on her." Mismatched readiness between sender and receiver results in messages that fail to connect.

3. Sophistication (obscurity): Sophistication in this context refers to a listener's awareness of a specific subject. What is the person's level of experience, education, and familiarity in a certain topic or field?

Another way of looking at this is the degree of obscurity in the message. How easily is the content understood? Is it vague, cryptic, or inconspicuous?[6] Your message's obscurity should match your listeners' sophistication. If you try to teach introductory algebra to a graduate math major, you're going to get boredom, resistance, and rejection (high sophistication, low obscurity). Likewise, if you try to teach advanced calculus to a freshman algebra class, you'll see everyone wander into dreamland (low sophistication, high obscurity).

The primary goal of preaching is to connect with people where they are spiritually and take them to the next level. Too much review creates boredom. When you go over material that people have heard all their lives, they will disengage mentally. Effective communicators design messages appropriate to the sophistication levels of the receivers.

I remember giving a talk at a Leadership Training Network event on getting people involved in ministry. I thought I delivered an instructional and inspirational message. But

> *The better you know your audience, the better you can design a message that connects.*

when the feedback forms came back a few days later, I was disappointed. While I may have *presented* well, I had failed to *communicate* well. I had underestimated the sophistication of the crowd. These people did not need to be sold on the importance of getting people involved in ministry. They were pastors, staff, and congregational leaders who had already bought into the idea. They were ready for more advanced motivation, instruction, and idea development. I'd failed to connect with my audience because I had not invested enough time understanding their level of sophistication with the topic.

Readiness and sophistication are the two most ignored audience characteristics regarding message design. They affect each other. Note the following matrix:

	Low SOPHISTICATION	**High** SOPHISTICATION
READINESS High	**A. Overachiever** Don't spend time selling me. Don't overwhelm me. Start simple. Don't assume we understand.	**B. Professional** No preliminaries; "Go!" Keep stories minimal. Concepts rule. Dense content is fine.
READINESS Low	**C. Mass Audience** You'd better engage me. How can I benefit from this? Time is precious. Don't overwhelm me.	**D. Underachiever** Been there, done that. What is different/unique? Don't dumb down to me. What don't I know?

A. High readiness, low sophistication: Fun crowd. They are motivated to learn. Don't waste time selling the material, but also avoid taking advantage of this high readiness by giving them too much, causing them to choke on the content and, thus, diminishing their enthusiasm. Reward progress and gradually increase content as sophistication increases. Examples: new Christians interested in discipleship, spiritually oriented people with little experience in church life who are exploring Christianity.

B. High readiness, high sophistication: Great potential. This is a dynamic audience, ready to employ what they have learned and go to the next level. Don't waste a lot of effort in selling the need, long preliminaries, or engaging graphics or illustrations. Dense, complex content is preferred. Examples: physicians attending a medical conference, veteran believers who are truly mature in faith, pastors in change scenarios attending a church-change workshop.

C. Low readiness, low sophistication: Naive, ignorant, or neutral. These people are not motivated to hear. They are also unable to make an educated response because they are not familiar with the message. They need to be sold on how they can benefit from the message and then given content in bite-size chunks so that they learn without choking. Low density and simple content are preferred. Illustrate, repeat, and provide feedback/question-answer time where able. Examples: typical Easter/Christmas service crowds, senior pastors attending a technology conference.

D. Low readiness, high sophistication: Tough crowd. They know it all. You'll need to appropriately persuade them that they might gain more, that they may have missed something in the past, or that they may have failed to benefit fully from what they already know. Many of these people exist in traditional churches, making it a challenge for communicators to build excitement and learning. Examples: veteran Christians who have head knowledge but heart coolness, churched people with a bad church experience in their past, senior pastors attending a workshop on teaching children.

4. Context expectation: What are people expecting when they are preparing to receive your communication? While we deliver messages with a goal in mind, we must realize that receivers usually have

36

their own expectations regarding the message. When we fail to match these, we run the risk of disconnecting. Are they expecting education/information, inspiration/motivation, persuasion/selling, or entertainment/experience? Each of these assumptions creates different inner demands and attitudes within the audience. If they are coming to be modestly entertained, then spending too much effort on instruction will frustrate them.

Worship services often can be categorized by which of these expectations they address. For example, some services are primarily designed for audiences wanting inspiration or motivation. This in no way suggests that authentic Bible teaching does not take place there, but the services are not designed to focus on heavy content as much as an overall uplifting experience. Conversely, many Bible churches pride themselves in the amount of Bible education/information that is dispensed. More entertainment/experiential venues attract spectators and those who want to be immersed in an experience. Most evangelists are known for focusing on persuasion/selling. Any given service might cross these boundaries, but these match general audience expectations. Churches tend to attract people who are searching for a specific experience.

A common error is to overestimate the motivation and sophistication of an audience. Begin simply and work up.

If you dropped a typical Bible teaching message into an inspiration service, people would be frustrated by the focus on head over heart. Conversely, trying to inspire or promote an experience in a traditional Bible church service will create a similar degree of frustration. This is why some conservative churches consider Pentecostals as having sacrificed the Bible for "experience," while some Pentecostals view conservatives as having a dead faith.

The primary reason for this is differing expectations. Romance movie attendees want a romance, not an action film, sci-fi, or documentary. When you sign up to attend an informational meeting about a time share in order to claim an outlandish prize, only to find out it is really a cover for a high pressure sales presentation, you'll be irritated. Bait-and-switch communication—setting an expectation that does not match the content—

closes down communication. Knowing the audience's expectations helps a sender design messages that are most apt to connect with receivers.

5. *Diversity:* The more homogeneous the audience in terms of demographics, sophistication, readiness, and expectations, the easier it is to design a message. One size can fit all. The more diverse your audience, the more difficult it becomes to reach everyone. You generally need to move toward the most common denominator within the group. Natural communicators do this intuitively after some initial investigation and observation. Some communicators only speak with specific audience types because they are effective at targeting a certain group well. The best communicators are flexible enough to respond appropriately to a diverse number of groups.

Politicians are renowned for talking without saying anything. A primary reason is that their receivers are so diverse. It is a challenge to connect well with any one individual in the audience because they're shooting for everyone. Speakers who have only one style but try to communicate with too much diversity are usually ineffective. We've all heard speakers like that. Obviously, the communicator failed to understand the audience—or you were not one of the people he had in mind when he was designing the message.

HOW TO DISCOVER THESE CHARACTERISTICS

Here are ten suggestions for getting and staying in touch with your most common message receivers. Some of these ideas are national in perspective, but the best ones for you are going to be quite local. The most effective places to discover clues to your local culture lie within a twenty-minute drive of your church. Don't invest a lot of time in any one of these ideas. The goal is to graze quickly, creating a mental collage of what people in your area think, feel, and do.

1. Interview and survey people in your target market who represent your bull's-eye. Imagine a radio station that played three country songs, followed by three classical music tunes, then three rock, three contemporary Christian, three polka, and three big band songs. It would have no listeners. No church can reach everyone in its community. Those that do best know whom God has called them to primarily reach.

When you have determined this for your church, talk to people within this group. Buy these people a meal and listen to their hopes, hurts, dreams, values, and frustrations. Invite them to a forum where, as a group, they can tell you their concerns, felt needs, and goals in life. You can also pretest members to see how much they know about a subject (sophistication) and survey their interests and attitudes (readiness).

2. *Review secular media,* focusing on major topics, graphics, and ads. Spending fifteen minutes at a magazine rack every week or two is a good start. One of my personal current favorites is Fast Company, which portrays the new business paradigm. Although you can read many of its articles online, I prefer the hard-copy version because, in addition to the articles, the ads reveal current attitudes with edgy graphics and creative marketing approaches. Satire, humor, and in-your-face thinking pervade. Scan local newspapers for major themes, articles, and even editorials. Surf the Internet for sites that market to people in your area, or ask your audience members what sites they frequent.

3. *Channel surf once a week.* I can hear the guys now: "Just doing audience analysis, hon. The book said I should channel surf." The goal is to keep in touch with what a majority of your audience is doing on any given night of the week. Look briefly at popular shows and ads. If you want to understand the children's culture, watch the Disney Channel. If you want to better know what youth and young adults are thinking and dealing with, check into MTV. Adults cue in on Letterman and Leno. Don't watch to find out what to slam in next Sunday's lesson but to see what your audience and their peers are watching (and likely buying into). Notice language, jokes, dress, hairstyles, conversation themes, and other nuances. Take advantage of advertisers' huge marketing research budgets by watching what ads have to say and how they say it.

4. *Go to the movies.* This may not sound like very spiritual advice. While many of us attend for our own entertainment, an additional reason to buy a movie ticket is to understand what your people are seeing, feeling, and thinking. If you hear several people comment on a movie they saw, it might be worth a look—not so much for your personal enjoyment but to experience what they are being exposed to. Obviously, this has appropriate limits, but movies are expressions of our culture as well as influences on our society.

5. *Review these four sections in your popular, local, non-Christian bookstore: bestsellers, business, self-help, and religion (spirituality).* These will give you a good idea of what others are reading because books now have shorter shelf lives than ever before, so popular bookstores tend to carry the titles that sell best in their areas. After you do this a few times, subsequent visits will only last a few moments as you scan for new books and thematic shifts.

6. *Beef up on applicable research.* Gallup and Barna Research are my favorites, but there are other books, seminars, and study results that provide insight into cultural norms and values. Make sure to look for current reports, as our culture keeps changing rapidly. You'll learn which church and secular writers seem to have good grasps on cultural norms and social trends.

7. *Do on-location message prep.* After doing research, one of the things I have come to enjoy is taking my laptop to a local mall or restaurant and crafting my Sunday message there. While the ambient noise may distract some of us, it's a helpful process to "take it to the street" and ponder how other people would think about the words we write. "Would the woman who just walked by understand the concepts? Would those guys laugh, scratch their heads, say I'm 'full of it,' or fall asleep?" Getting outside the walls of the church brings a reality check to message design, as you imagine what people sitting and walking around you would think of your words.

8. *Do mall observations.* The new town centers are shopping malls, where people gather as much to socialize as to shop. This is an optimum place to see a lot of people in a short amount of time. Find a convenient coffee shop or cafe and people watch. Go at different times—noon, evening, and weekend—and see how they dress and talk and where they go.

9. *Employ secret shoppers.* In *The Five Star Church* (Regal, 1999), I talk about improving quality by hiring people who represent the people you're trying to reach and paying them to visit your church and provide feedback after the service. If you're serious about improving your communication, employ outsiders to critique your messages—live, by tape, or even by written transcript. Ask for details regarding things that made sense and those that did not.

10. Provide anonymous feedback systems. Everyone's a critic, so why not take advantage of that by learning what hits a homer and what strikes out in your messages? Don't rely on foyer comments because people in church tend to be nice and think of each other as family. They're most apt to tell you what puts them in the best light with you, not what they discuss over lunch. Anonymous feedback loops provide focused information on what did and did not make sense. But remember, all feedback is not equal in value. The best advice is to survey those whom you're most interested in reaching. (See Chapter 9 for more on feedback gathering.)

> *The Incarnation increased God's connectivity with people. Likewise, we communicators are best when we are members of the audience. Reduce the distance from pulpit to pew.*

The senior pastor loved to bounce sermon ideas off his associate.

⊐━━━━ Discussion/Thought Prompters ━━━━⊏

1. Why is it the sender's responsibility to get inside the receiver's head?
2. What do you think are the most common sermon or church teaching problems? How can better audience analysis help alleviate these?
3. What is the makeup of your typical audience? your target audience/person? How and why do these differ?
4. Can you think of a time a popular speaker missed the mark in terms of relating to his or her audience? Analyze it. What happened? How would you advise the person to improve?
5. How can you improve your audience analysis?

Chapter Three
Secret #3

Clarify
the Context

GETTING A GRIP ON CONTEXT

O K, let me shoot straight with you. This is a messy chapter. I'll take the blame for part of it, but to be honest, the concept of context avoids pretty bows and ribbons. Context is about culture, emotions, intangibles, and mental mud. We'll discuss some very practical "to-do" matters, but hang in there with me for the next few pages because, while context is messy, it's a key ingredient to creating messages that connect. We have no written record of Jesus ever using a canned approach to evangelism or kingdom talk. He knew that one size doesn't fit all. As the context changes, so must the messages we use to connect. Some communicators may seem to succeed with a similar message over and over, but that's primarily because they attract similar audiences and seek (or create) the same context in which that message works. But when the context changes, you have to design a different approach.

If there's one thing we preachers get drilled into us in seminary and ministerial preparation, it is how crucial context is to understanding biblical meanings—and rightly so. Who said what, to whom, and for what reason are integral to understanding. Even the best of us have perused the tabloids as we wait our turn in the grocery store or drugstore line. Photos, quotes, and news stories are often taken out of context, creating

43

Understanding both biblical and contemporary contexts is vital for designing messages that connect.

completely misleading and controversial sugges-tions. Gossip is typically content with an element of truth placed in a different context. Context can be *more* important than the content. That's why repeat-ing a story is so difficult; re-creating context is next to impossible.

Prooftexting is a popular example of trying to make the Bible appear to support what you're say-ing. While your underlying premise may be correct, a biblical passage taken out of context is not valid support for that premise. For example, context is what makes so much of the book of Job difficult for preach-ing. Several chapters consist of godly sounding lectures given by Job's friends to confront his suffering (4, 5, 8, 11, 15, 18, 20, 22, 25, 32–37). When you read them out of context, they seem theologically correct and beneficial. But after these friends' self-righteous feedback, God tells them that they're all wet. They've misdiagnosed Job's malady, assuming it to be a spiritual illness in Job's heart (38–41). "Who is this that darkens my counsel with words without knowledge?" (Job 38:2). The New Century Version says, "Who is this that makes my purpose unclear by saying things that are not true?"

Words without knowledge? Darkening God's counsel? Things that aren't true? What a rude awakening for Job's support group! They thought they'd hit the bull's-eye, but God said they missed the target completely. Most of us have been there and done that, giving spiritual-sounding advice that did not fit the situation.

I've probably not told you anything new about context as a pas-tor/preacher. But I belabor this point because just as we must strive to uncover the historical meaning of a text, so must we learn to read the contemporary context of the message we're preparing.

"Context: The parts...which precede or follow a word, sentence, or passage, and affect its meaning...The surrounding environment, circum-stance, or facts which help give a total picture of something."[1]

What precedes your message? What current events have taken place in your country, your community, and the individual lives of your audience? Who are these people? What do they care about? What are they aloof toward? Why did they come to hear you? Are they there voluntarily or involuntarily? What is their history individually, together, and within their community? What's your experience with them and/or people like them? What are their struggles? What motivates them? Are they generally self-satisfied, broken, depressed, joyful, or complacent?

With those answers in mind, think of what you want to accomplish with your message. What potential barriers are you facing to deliver it?

Demographic factors we discussed in Chapter 2 are part of context, too. In what stage of life are your listeners? Are they single, married with small kids, teens, empty nesters, retired? What is their ethnicity? Are they lower income, middle income, or upper income? Is the community urban, suburban, rural, or a mixture? Is the local economy up or down? What obvious or hidden filters are going to bias what they hear or read? Are they new to the faith or veterans? Are they authentic Christians or merely churched? Are they mature in the Lord or just old?

Many message designers ignore their own personal context. But you cannot separate the message from the messenger. Where are you in life compared to your audience? Do you relate to them? Do they relate to you? Are you preoccupied with other concerns right now, or are you focused? What does the content of this message mean to you personally? If it is merely a professional speech, chances are it will sound tinny, like clanging an empty coffee can.

How is your soul? Are you harboring a secret sin? Is your marriage frayed? Are you preoccupied with financial, health, parenting, or family matters? Do you feel like getting out of the ministry? You can compensate for messenger malaise occasionally, but most of the time, it will diminish your effectiveness. (A possible exception is when your present pain relates specifically to audience angst.)

What is likely to follow your message? Will the world in which you live be the same, or is it changing? As your audience thinks about the future, what are their fears, their dreams, and the probabilities of realizing them? What problems might they face if they respond to the particular call your message is making?

Where are you going to be in the lives of these people after they receive your message? Are you a local pastor living among his or her parishioners or a special speaker who will blow out of town with the next wind? Do you pastor a "church of the revolving door," or will you likely live, retire, and die among these saints? Discovering the context of your audience means answering a lot of questions.

CONTEXT METAPHORS

Getting to the root of the concept of *context* is difficult because it's primarily intangible and cultural. Here are a few word pictures to better establish the role of context.

Context as lens: I dropped by the vacant lot to check out a man who was selling sunglasses from the back of his van. He explained these were third-generation BluBlockers, a type of sunglasses that remove glare without making things look dark. Context is like colored lenses that tint everything we see, hear, and think.

Context as spice: Ever taste nursing-home food? Add a little salt, pepper, and seasoning, and it's not too bad. Some cultures always add curry to their foods, others use cilantro, and yet others use garlic. Context flavors the information that comes into our lives, taking bland data and transforming it into meaningful messages. Effective messengers are to communication what fine chefs are to food.

Context as attire: Do you wear the same clothes to go to church on Sunday as you do to work on your car or clean your garage? Does your spouse dress differently for a hot date than to take the kids to meet the new principal? (We hope so.) Context determines what the content is wearing. There's a big difference between gym shorts and a tuxedo. Your perception of people will vary based on what they are wearing, even though the person underneath is the same. Likewise, your listeners' perception of your message will vary based on the context surrounding it.

Context as backdrop: Did you ever buy furniture from a showroom, only to take it home and discover that it doesn't look the same in your living room? That's why one person's couch looks great with his or her décor but would clash with yours. Colonial, Mediterranean, Tudor, ranch, and territorial style homes all look good in the right setting but odd in the wrong part of the country. Context is the backdrop of our lives.

Context isn't just based on broad emotional and cultural considerations. There are also elements specific to you, particularly

- the setting and purpose of your message,
- environmental influences, and
- the relationship of the speaker with the audience.

SETTING AND PURPOSE OF THE MESSAGE

What is the setting of your message?

A funeral homily should look and sound different from one for a wedding. Presenting the same sermon to a group of junior high campers that you did for last Sunday's adult congregation is going to go over like the proverbial lead balloon. The Rotary Club is not a Sunday school class. Chances are you can't prepare a seminar for pastors that would fit a group of elementary school teachers.

But it's not just differing groups of people; the same people in different settings create unique demands on message preparation. When physicians come to church, they don't expect a medical talk and would likely be disappointed if they received it. Conversely, preaching to them at a medical conference would not fit. Although most of us consistently communicate in the same setting week after week, proper message design requires that we seriously take into account that setting—especially when it changes.

ENVIRONMENTAL INFLUENCES

The setting is an intangible aspect of context, dealing with the reasons people came together. A more tangible part of context is the immediate physical environment. We are not bodies with souls; we are souls with bodies. We must consider the physical and affective side of communication because surroundings influence the context in which we receive a message. Communicators who connect understand the importance of aesthetics. Anyone can make a cup of coffee, but Starbucks has made millions of dollars by providing a little ambience with that cup of java. Pretending

> *"We shape our buildings; thereafter they shape us."*
> —WINSTON CHURCHILL[2]

The "rule" that a church will plateau once it reaches 80 percent of its seating capacity is really a myth. It may be true for parking, but people like to feel that they're at a place that's happening, popular, and full. People hear best when crowded. Boomers and busters tend to travel in herds. Urbanization and the boom of megachurches over the last ten to twenty years demonstrate this.

that the only thing that matters is message content suggests that we're detached from our culture. Let's look at several creature-comfort issues that can make or break effective communication, even though they appear to have little to do with message design.

Seating

Comfort: Hard, wooden pews are being replaced by ergonomically designed theater chairs. The old saying tells us the brain cannot endure more than the seat can withstand. If people are distracted by uncomfortable seating, you'll diminish your ability to connect, even if only slightly. Some restaurants provide hard chairs in order to turn tables because people won't sit on hard chairs for very long.

Crowding: Critical mass can make or break message response. People who listen to a presenter in a packed room consistently rate the speech higher than those hearing the same talk in a moderately filled room, and higher yet than in a room that has many open chairs. Two of the most common energy killers are empty chairs and too much open space.

People in the audience take cues from each other. They unconsciously play off one another. Room psychology is important to message reception. It is always better to set up additional chairs if necessary than to let people spread out in an auditorium. Remove chairs, rope off back pews, or do whatever it takes to keep people at 70 to 90 percent of perceived capacity. If you have a big room and movable chairs, put more space between rows and seats to give it a fuller feel. Let them fly first class versus coach. Don't underestimate the power of appearance. A crowded room gives the impression that there's something here worth coming for, so "I'd better not miss it." Some people rebel against being told where they can and cannot sit, but if the benefits are explained to them, most will comply. Say something like "Studies prove that people get more out of the message when they sit together instead of spread out over a room, so for the sake of your soul and others', please help us by avoiding the roped-off sections. Thank you."

The effect of crowding has a lot to do with critical mass, a social phenomenon that creates energy, momentum, and a sense of well-being. Service elements may be done excellently, but if the audience does not reach a size that creates its own sense of thriving, the service will likely languish. The size of critical mass varies from event to event, but intentional crowding and spacing can lower the perceived number to obtain it.

Arrangement: After you do enough seminars in hotel conference rooms, you realize most room planners don't understand effective communication. They often set up straight rows in long, narrow halls. The best layout is a semicircle so that attention is on the presenter but people can interact with each other and feel a part of community via their peripheral vision.

Temperature: If it's in your capabilities, make sure room temperature is well within the comfort zone. A bit too cool is better than a bit too warm because heat deadens our senses, lulling us to sleep or making us irritable. Body heat raises room temperature, so if you're crowding your seating area, make sure you adequately cool the room ahead of time on warm days.

Distractions: Cell phones, crying babies, traffic noise, people coming and going, and countless other distractions during your communication can lower your connectivity. Although speakers tend to notice these more than the audience, controlling distractions as much as possible is important if you want to increase your effectiveness.

Proximity: In the old days, preachers stood behind huge, holy furnishings—"A Mighty Fortress Is Our Pulpit." Fortunately, most of us have given up opaque pulpits for acrylic ones, skinny music stands, or even none at all. Body language and mobility are great connecting factors, so the more you can do to feel close to your audience, the better. This is especially important when people are more than fifty feet from the speaker. Larger auditoriums project the communicator onto screens to give the appearance that the speaker is close to the hearers and to maximize facial expressions and body gestures. Be as physically close to the audience as possible. Some speakers do not feel comfortable walking among the congregation, and line of sight issues may not allow it. But when stage height, altars, empty front rows, and other furnishings create spatial barriers, connectivity declines. Physical distance creates emotional distance.

Lighting: Today's experts vary in their opinions on what lighting makes for a great speaking setting. Early twentieth-century churches avoided outside distractions by not using translucent stained glass or by having no auditorium windows at all. When overhead projectors and video began to be used, lights needed to be dimmed in order to see these images, but current video equipment with more lumens can now work in brighter auditoriums. Some churches like darker settings, while others prefer brighter ones. Either way, the speaker always needs to be well-illuminated. Shadows and dark spots on the stage reduce the audience's ability to see facial gestures and keep its attention on the speaker.

The upside to a dark audience is that distractions are lessened and people focus more on the speaker because their eyes are drawn to light. It also can feel safer to seekers who can watch a presenter in virtual anonymity, much as they would a movie or concert act. But the downside of a darker audience area seems to outweigh the advantages. When the auditorium is dark, the communicator has a difficult time making eye contact with people and tends to emotionally disconnect from his or her hearers. Note-taking is a way of engaging the audience but is greatly reduced when lights are low. We've already mentioned the value of listeners interacting with each other emotionally, and this is also minimized when it is too dark for them to see each other.

Sound: Screechy feedback, static, and low fidelity public address systems decrease message connectivity. If people cannot hear a speaker, then there is no chance to respond. If they are distracted by poor sound quality, they will not be concentrating on the message. Wireless technology allows us the opportunity to be mobile, not tied down by fixed microphones or long, black cables. Do whatever it takes to procure adequate audio fidelity that delivers high quality sound without drawing attention to itself. Finding a competent person to run the system...well, that's a more difficult matter.

Aesthetics: Coffee shops, grocery stores, gas stations, hotels, malls, and office buildings are putting more and more money and effort into first appearances and attractive facades and interiors. Packaging often costs more than the product it contains.

While guest speakers have little control over the décor of their surroundings, lead pastors can influence the affective side of the environment in which they communicate. Color, graphics, textures, space, stage, and room layouts influence emotional impact. Professional decorators and space designers can significantly improve the feel of a speaking area, heightening the sense of importance and quality. People associate experiences with the surroundings.

Attire: What is appropriate attire? The old rule of thumb is that the speaker should dress as well as the best-dressed person in the audience because many people find it more difficult to ascribe credibility to and develop rapport with those who are not as well-dressed as they are. Sometimes, though, a speaker needs a certain style of attire to promote a desired attitude or even portray a specific persona. A better contemporary rule is to dress according to the majority of those in the audience.

When I moved from a seeker church in Southern California to a large, institutional church in the Midwest, I unknowingly broke a local attire rule. I'd worn polo shirts on Sundays in California but knew that suits were traditional in this church. The first Sunday I wore a nice tan suit. I was soon informed that appropriate attire was a *dark* suit with a plain white shirt. Oops.

My wife was the first female on the pastoral staff at a large church in Southern California and was encouraged not to wear red dresses on the platform as they added too much color. There are few rational reasons for wearing what we do, but I guarantee that attire can add to or detract from message connectivity. Rules of thumb regarding speaker attire include:

- Dress similarly to the majority of your audience.
- Don't wear clothing that draws attention to itself.
- If you have a specific target group within your audience, strive to look like those in that group—unless the look is too divergent from who you are personally and the audience would perceive you as inauthentic.

RELATIONSHIP BETWEEN SPEAKER AND AUDIENCE (CPR: CREDIBILITY, PERSONALITY, RAPPORT)

The audience's perception of the speaker is a vital part of the communication context. Three primary communicator factors influence your message's connectivity.

Credibility: Who said, "The primary purpose of an individual is to help others discover their destiny in life"? Abraham Lincoln, Confucius, Billy Graham, or Saddam Hussein? As far as I know, none of them said this, but do you see how the name you affix to the quote influences your reaction to it? Audiences add value to messages that are deemed credible. After a ministry leader's moral failure is revealed, his subsequent messages may be the same as before the revelation, but they are devalued.

"We disbelieve our newspaper, our priests and preachers, and our political business leaders—and one another. Fifty-five percent of Americans in 1960 agreed that 'most people can be trusted.' By 2000 only 34 percent did."[4]

"Prospects do not buy how good you are at what you do. They buy how good you are *at who you are*."[5]

> On the Sabbath, [Jesus] gave a lecture in the meeting place. He made a real hit, impressing everyone. "We had no idea he was this good!" they said. "How did he get so wise all of a sudden, get such ability?"
> But in the next breath they were cutting him down: "He's just a carpenter—Mary's boy. We've known him since he was a kid. We know his brothers, James, Justus, Jude, and Simon, and his sisters. Who does he think he is?" They tripped over what little they knew about him and fell, sprawling. And they never got any further.
> Jesus told them, "A prophet has little honor in his hometown, among his relatives, on the streets he played in as a child." Jesus wasn't able to do much of anything there (Mark 6:2-5, *The Message*).

Communication is enhanced when we can improve our credibility, real and perceived.

Personality: Communicators come in all thirty-one flavors. There's not much you can do to change your natural wiring. Just be aware that you will connect with some and not others, in part based on nothing other than a receiver's perception of your temperament. There are people sitting side by side who hear the same words but respond to them differently based on whether or not they like your personality. "The speaker is too uptight; no fun." "He's a control freak who acts like he knows it all." "She's too giddy and animated for me." "He's too mellow; add some passion." Play to your strengths and be yourself, but realize we all have limitations in this department.

> *Personal credibility is critical to spiritual communication, but it's not everything. You have to have it to play the game, but it doesn't guarantee a win.*

Rapport: Personality differences aside, communicators can enhance their connectivity by establishing rapport with their receivers. Far too many pastors sneak into the worship service from backstage during the opening musical number instead of "working the crowd" beforehand. Shaking hands, being visible, smiling, joking around, welcoming people, and "slapping backs and kissing babies," as one friend of mine suggests, are means of enhancing rapport before a message is presented. Although some pastors cannot justify this for various reasons, warming up to a crowd prior to a presentation also helps you discern the spirit, attitudes, and energy level in advance so you can make minor adjustments to your message to compensate appropriately. Telling a joke, sharing a personal story, and humble but genuine greetings are all means of gaining rapport with receivers.

TO COMPROMISE OR NOT TO COMPROMISE—THAT IS THE QUESTION

Some people think you have to water down the truth if you want to engage people today. Let's look at Jesus' example. Jesus tended to be unconventional in the way he taught. He was a master communicator. The unconventional church zealots of his day chastised him for his out-of-the-box approach to ministry, not to mention his theology and praxis

> *People do not reject the gospel as much as they do the way we present it.*

(theory put to practice). If we follow the style of Jesus' teaching ministry, we will likely find ourselves communicating in a way that neither compromises our content nor disconnects with our receivers. When people confuse principles with methodology, content with presentation, and essence with form, they will inevitably get sidetracked by matters that create needless conflict. *Jesus was very conservative with his standards but very liberal in his approach to people.* This conservative/liberal dynamic is at times a precarious tightrope to walk.

There is no need to water down the gospel in order to communicate with people, but you can't slice off a pound of beefsteak and expect most to swallow it whole. A teaspoon of medicine can be enough to gag a bull, so we should not confuse potency with the size of the dosage. Most parents learn how to give medicine to toddlers. They mix it with a fruit or vegetable or—even better—a popular treat. The children get the medicine in a way they will swallow.

At the same time, the idea that all medicine tastes bad is no longer true. Those of us forty-somethings who've confronted our middle-age spread have discovered a whole array of nutritional products that are low in carbohydrates, fat, and sugar but taste relatively good. Challenging messages that are skillfully crafted can deliver confrontational truths in a manner that demonstrates love and can be swallowed.

Old-style preachers assume that if something tastes good or feels right, then it can't be the gospel truth. It's true that there are some sermons that feel good but are watered down and spiritually impotent, but we can't lump every inoffensive message into that same category. Freshman logic taught us that all fathers are men but not all men are fathers. Watered-down sermons don't offend, but not all inoffensive messages are watered down. Effective spiritual doctors must learn new ways to get their patients to take their meds and pursue health. Hitting people over the head with a God-bat does not work like it used to in America. We must be more subtle, intentional, and sophisticated, but we can still consistently deliver a powerful punch in a manner that is forthright, genuine, and biblical.

Preachers are primarily concerned about the context of specific biblical passages. Communicators are concerned about both the context of the Scripture and the context of the message they're preparing. As we said before, good communicators tend to develop a style that makes them effective in certain contexts. Great communicators are able to adapt to a variety of contexts. They'll change delivery style, content, density, and a variety of other factors in order to connect with the audience in that specific context.

More narrow-minded folks would want you to think, "If it ain't expository, it ain't preachin'." Expository preaching lets Scripture set the agenda for the topic to be discussed and then sheds light on the selected passage. Our job as "exposers" is to adequately research the terms, historical settings, and sociological nuances of the passages. Topical preaching, on the other hand, lets audience felt needs and life-flow set the agenda for the topic. As communicators, our responsibility is to make sure we address these matters with wisdom that does not compromise scriptural truth. Both are viable styles.

Jesus communicated topically, addressing life situations that arose. When he was tempted, he quoted Scriptures as part of his response to the devil (Matthew 4). Jesus intrigued a mature, religious intellectual with

Pastor Doug Tedbull doesn't have a clue.

Used by artist's permission. Reprinted from Leadership Journal.

the idea of being born a second time (John 3). A setting at a well turned into a backdrop for discussing spiritual water (John 4). Paul presented a very sensitive, apologetic message to the people of Athens (Acts 17).

The logical push-back is that Jesus and Paul were not so much unpacking known Scriptures as they were actually creating Scripture by their teaching and writing. Ironically, we do not have a good biblical model for what it means to actually prepare a biblical message. Those who suggest there is one right way to preach or teach are speaking far more from tradition than they are a biblical guideline. This is not to suggest that "anything goes," merely that there is an array of appropriate styles and methods for conveying God's Word.

Clarifying the context of the message involves accurate assessment of the setting and background in which the message will be presented. While natural communicators do this intuitively, we all can do much to enhance our effectiveness in connecting with those we serve with our messages.

Discussion/Thought Prompters

1. What's the most helpful thing you learned from Secret #3?
2. What do you see as the most challenging factor in bridging biblical context with audience context?
3. Describe your most common communication context in terms of setting, audience, expectations, physical conditions, and so on.
4. Which of your environmental concerns can you address to enhance connectivity?
5. Why do you agree or disagree with the idea that you don't have to compromise the gospel in order to connect with people today?

Chapter Four
Secret #4

Strategize the Four Primary Message-Design Components

The next secret of effective communication is directly related to context and involves strategizing the four main message-design elements. These include the message goal, content mass, time allotment, and audience constellation.

MESSAGE GOAL

Want to ruin the multi-billion–dollar National Basketball Association in one simple action? Easy! Just take the metal rings off the backboards. The goal of basketball is to get the ball through the hoop. Remove the goal, and the game becomes a meaningless series of dribbling and passing on a wooden court.

What is the goal of your message? Many speakers take their audiences for a ride but never get anywhere because they don't know where they're going. They have little sense of destination or purpose. Messages that connect have a clear sense of direction toward a goal. What do you plan to achieve? The four primary goals of messages align with the four types of audience expectation we listed in Chapter 2: informing, inspiring, persuading, and entertaining.

Informing: dispensing new knowledge in order to educate and deepen understanding.

If you don't know what you want to achieve, you won't know how to get there.

Inspiring: elevating a person's attitude or feelings about a cause or belief.

Persuading: convincing people to act on an idea; motivating toward behavioral change.

Entertaining: engaging for amusement, relaxation, and enjoyment.

Message design begins with a goal in mind and ends up by asking the questions "Did we accomplish this goal?" and "How do we know if we did or did not?" When our objectives are muddy and convoluted, the outcomes are likely to reflect this. While you can use a variety of means to accomplish your message's goal, the more focused your objective is, the more likely you are to create a message that connects. For example, you can use entertainment as a means to inspire, but if inspiration is your goal, you'll design your message differently than if it is merely to entertain. *Sesame Street's* goal was to inform (teach) preschoolers, but they used entertainment as a fun way to engage the kids as they learned numbers, alphabet, and other concepts. Most movies are pure entertainment, but many people use movie clips in church services these days, not to entertain but to illustrate biblical points.

Goals affect design.

Informational messages concern themselves with explaining content—including things like historical background and cultural significance—and how such factors influence each other. Teaching is not merely dumping information. It also explains how that information applies to the receivers. While learning is often an inspirational process, it's not the primary objective. Teaching preachers like Greg Laurie and Charles Stanley primarily design informational messages.

Persuasive messages look for the sale, even though they may inform, entertain, and inspire as means to that end. When you plan to get a commitment, you'll want to focus on persuasion. Whether it's a salesman pitching a car or a pastor leading a stewardship campaign, touching the heart in order to influence free will is the goal. Josh McDowell, Billy Graham, and other evangelists primarily design persuasive messages.

Inspirational messages move us emotionally. People get beat up, lose hope, burn out, and seek motivation to persevere. While some pastors devalue the importance of inspirational messages, they are more needed than you might think. Zig Ziglar and Robert Schuller are known for inspirational messages.

Entertainment is a justifiable ministry objective. Most spectator-oriented Christian music (versus participative worship), Christian comedy, plays, movies, and Christian fiction have the objective of entertaining. Providing a God-oriented alternative to secular entertainment is a valid purpose and may have the side effects of inspiration, persuasion, and information.

Know which one to use.

Deciding on a message goal is not always easy. An adept designer can create different messages from the same text or topic. The message designer's discernment, the guidance of the Holy Spirit, and sensing the needs of the receivers all influence the selection of a message goal. Speakers tend to develop style strengths so that some become known as teachers, others as inspirers, and still others as persuaders. Context often determines the goal of the message. The key is appropriateness to the situation. If you inform when persuasion is needed, you'll fail to connect as you should. If you inspire when teaching is desired, you'll be less effective.

As a general rule, informational/teaching messages are less complex and animated. They focus more on the intellectual aspect of thinking, often referred to as left-brain processes. People come with notebooks, pens, and Bibles, ready for longer messages. Inspirational messages tend to be more life-relevant, full of stories that touch the heart, like the *Chicken Soup for the Soul* series. Persuasive messages tend to focus on the heart and emotions but move toward a point of decision, either calling for a personal commitment or even a physical one such as walking to an altar, filling out a response card, or buying something. To inspire and persuade usually requires right-brain processes. An exception is apologetics, which is left-brain persuasive. The goals determine how you go about

> *"Every service ultimately sells an experience: the experience of receiving a service. But what is that experience?"*
> —Harry Beckwith[1]

Every message worth delivering deserves its own mission statement.

designing the messages, how you illustrate, how you begin and end, and the general format of the presentation.

Create a purpose statement for each message:

Pilots file flight plans, declaring beforehand their destination. One of the most helpful practices you can establish to begin your message design effectively is to write a purpose statement. Writing it down forces you to solidify your thinking, and it clarifies your commitment toward that goal. It also helps you hold yourself accountable to staying on course. For example, if you're teaching a series on the life of King David, an opening message based on 1 Samuel 17, dealing with David and Goliath, might have a purpose statement such as "This message is designed to *persuade* people to trust God more, based on David's encounter with the giant Philistine." The purpose statement should clarify the objective in a single sentence. Within this message you may inform, inspire, and entertain as means, but at the end, a persuasive message will usually call for a commitment. It may be a call to make a decision for Christ or a commitment to deepen one's faith in a specific area. As an immediate action step, you might ask people to write down a "giant" in their lives and commit that problem to prayer. That same text could be used for an informative message to show people how faith changes our responses to difficult situations. It could also be used for an inspirational message, inspiring people to risk trusting God in adverse circumstances.

CONTENT MASS

How much does your message weigh? Are the mental muscles of your audience capable of carrying it? Content mass includes a variety of factors that affect a message's weight and thickness—an important part of message design.

Info chunk: A piece of information that stands by itself is considered an info chunk. Remember outlining in English class? Each main point of an outline should represent a single chunk of info. Lower level bullets in the outline elaborate on that main point but should not add weight.

The lower levels may be made up of subpoints, which divide the main point, or supports, which amplify it.[2] In general, subpoints are more left-brain oriented. They serve to break the point into more bite-size pieces. A support may be repetition, paraphrase, description, explanation, quotation, numerical data, illustration, contrast, comparison, definition, or visual support. Supports tend to provide redundancy to ease the mental strain of processing an abstract point. They also provide concreteness, vividness, and specificity. Both help the audience connect with the main info chunks in a more memorable way.

The Law of 5±2 (5 plus or minus 2 = 3 to 7): A typical Sunday message that has the best chances of connecting will have approximately three to seven info chunks. When you go over seven, you're apt to overwhelm your receivers and reduce the effectiveness of your message as each info chunk competes for attention with the others. If you use fewer than three, you're apt to underwhelm them, losing them to boredom. The running joke about typical sermons is that they're three points and illustrations. That's about right when you consider that the average congregation is a diverse cross section of the community and your time is limited to twenty-five to forty-five minutes. Speakers whose outlines contain a long list of points run the risk of diminishing the impact of the main points. The mind can only process so much info before it shuts down. The goal is not to be skinny or plump but just right.

Density: A law in physics tells us that all objects fall to earth at the same speed. Nevertheless, if someone drops objects from a window above you, it's better to be under a five-pound bag of feathers than a five-pound cannonball! The difference is that the metal cannonball is much more dense, with its weight jammed into a smaller space.

Message density has to do with the amount of information that is communicated in a certain allotment of time. The more info chunks in less time, the greater the message density. Add time and keep info chunks the same, and the message becomes less dense. A medical briefing for cardiologists on the latest techniques of angioplasty is likely to be very dense. You have a sophisticated group of motivated receivers who need little illustration or entertainment. On the other hand, if you're a cardiologist attempting to explain recent heart restoration practices to a group of high schoolers, you'll need to make it far less dense. Some refer to this as "dumbing it down," but we're just reducing the density in light of the current audience's sophistication and motivation, as well as time constraints.

Complexity: Complexity refers to the diversity of the message itself in terms of sensory stimulation. For example, a child playing "Chopsticks" with two fingers is presenting a simple musical message. A classical pianist doing an elaborate, sweeping rendition of "Chopsticks" would be apt to be far more complex. Adding layers of sensory stimulation raises complexity, while not necessarily increasing density. Multimedia has given us the ability to significantly increase message complexity. A thirty-second television ad during prime time is apt to have high complexity with low density. Mountain Dew's "Do the Dew" message is very light, with only one info chunk (drinking Dew is cool), but the message is complex as it is delivered with loud music, flashing images of extreme sporting events, and blaring graphics that grab our attention and raise our heart rates. Complex messages tend to engage us and can add to communication if designed well. They can also be distracting and detract from a message goal if used improperly.

Most Sunday morning preaching formats tend to be low complexity. The simple, talking-head format makes it difficult for media-oriented audiences to stay focused. Animated speaking or speaking more quickly helps. The use of visual aids, media, and other graphics raises the level of engagement.

During the first

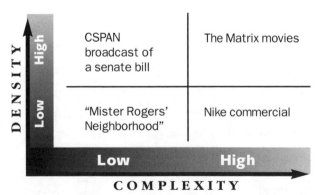

postmodern conference my wife and I attended, I noticed no less than five large video monitors in the room, each displaying a different array of images on them—most of which had nothing to do with the message theme or content. While the teacher spoke, people got up to get refreshments, do art projects at tables, and work on laptops. To us moderns, it smacked of a convention for those with attention deficits. Multilayered, complex messages will become more necessary to connect with younger people.

Info load: Estimating the load of a message is helpful in determining whether or not it is the right fit for a given audience. In order to estimate the information load of a message, you'll want to consider how obscure the message is to the audience, along with the number of info chunks. Remember, obscurity is to a message what sophistication is to an audience; the lower the sophistication, the higher the obscurity. On a 1 to 5 scale, 1 would be high obscurity, meaning the audience would find the information very difficult to understand; 3 would be moderate; and 5 would indicate easily understood content. The following graph can give you an idea of the info load of your message, once you've determined how many info chunks you have and the estimated obscurity of the message.[3]

INFO LOAD

AVERAGE OBSCURITY	INFO CHUNKS					
	>9	5–9	1–4			
3.37–5.0	5	3	1	ABOVE AVERAGE	7	Extremely
					6	Definitely
					5	Slightly
1.68–3.35	6	4	2		4	Average
					3	Slightly
1.0–1.67	7	5	3	BELOW AVERAGE	2	Definitely
					1	Extremely

Info load, density, and complexity determine content mass. Messages that connect contain the appropriate weight for the audience's sophistication and receptivity.

TIME ALLOTMENT

Preachers have some peculiar nightmares. They frequently involve sermons where people begin walking out on them or the service ends in some kind of depressing turmoil. When I was younger, my most common speaker-oriented bad dream was getting up to present and losing my notes. I was afraid I couldn't fill a half hour by winging it. The older I've gotten, the more I realize (both in writing and speaking) that my most difficult task is trying not to say too much. In message design, time is always a factor. You must consider how much time you have to say what to whom.

That's easier to say than to do. Some of the most difficult messages to design are the shortest because you have to make every moment count. Most of us work within defined time boundaries, whether it's a Sunday sermon, Bible study, seminar, or college class. If your weekly message is thirty minutes, you have time to moderately develop three to five info chunks, but not in great detail. When the audience is not familiar with your topic, you may only be able to develop one or two main points.

When you hear someone say, "That was over my head," it means you went too deep for that person and failed to connect. You can approximate the depth of your message in advance with a simple formula. The depth at which you dig is a matter of the number of info chunks (IC) you have, the amount of time allotted (TA), and audience sophistication (AS) on a scale from 1 to 10. If your audiences seem bored, try increasing your message depth. If they tell you it's over their heads, try lowering it.

$$\frac{IC \times TA}{AS} = \text{message depth}$$

There tends to be an inverse relationship between time and density when you're creating messages that connect. Patrick Marsh wrote, "We can reduce the duration of a message either by reducing the amount of information or by increasing the message's complexity [density]."[4] This gives the communicator leeway to be creative, but it can also mean more work. For example, if you know the content you want to deliver, designing it into an effective ten-minute devotional is often more difficult than doing so in a half-hour message. For the former, you must carefully craft every sentence. Advertisers often work months perfecting a sixty-second spot for the Super Bowl, not wanting to waste a second.

When time is short and sophistication is low, you have to dilute the message. If you pack too much into a message, you'll commit overload resulting in zero retention and, worse, a negative impression. If you run out of time, it's better to continue a series than try to overload it. But if you pack too little into a message, you'll bore your audience (and likely provoke critical feedback). Missing the mark in either way is poor communication stewardship. If you have no way of monitoring the motivation and sophistication of your audience members, lean toward erring on the side of simplicity. Again, speakers tend to assume a higher level of knowledge than the audience possesses. When in doubt, less is more.

You can intensify a message in less time by increasing complexity. Layering elements of sound, graphics, animation, and media allows you to communicate more in less time because you're tapping multiple senses. You're moving toward an experiential message. You also increase the breadth of people you connect with because some are audio learners, others visual, and a few tactile.

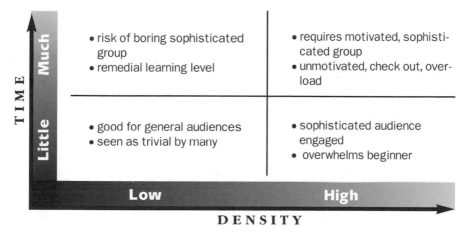

AUDIENCE CONSTELLATION

We tend to send messages the way we like to receive them. The reason professors are known for giving boring, academic, heady talks is because that's what they like. But when we speak out of our personal preferences instead of the audience's, we tend to connect less. It's not about us; it's about them.

My personal preference is communication that is fast-paced and pithy. When I am negatively critiqued, it's usually because I spoke too fast and tried to say too much. "Slow down," my wife tells me. "People need time to process. Don't try to give them so much." Effective message design is a selfless process. If you're unwilling to deny yourself and think of others, you'll diminish your connectivity.

"Do nothing out of selfish ambition or vain conceit, but in humility consider others better than yourselves. Each of you should look not only to your own interests, but also to the interests of others" (Philippians 2:3-4).

Here is the mantra of the effective communicator:

Even though I am free of the demands and expectations of everyone, I have voluntarily become a servant to any and all in order to reach a wide range of people: religious, nonreligious, meticulous moralists, loose-living immoralists, the defeated, the demoralized—whoever. I didn't take on their way of life. I kept my bearings in Christ—but I entered their world and tried to experience things from their point of view. I've become just about every sort of servant there is in my attempts to lead those I meet into a God-saved life (1 Corinthians 9:19-22, *The Message*).

This passage continues, which can be paraphrased for serious message designers as follows:

You've all been to the stadium and seen the athletes race. Everyone runs; one wins. Run to win. All good athletes train hard. They do it for a gold medal that tarnishes and fades. You're after one that's gold eternally.
 I don't know about you, but [I want to communicate to connect]. I'm giving it everything I've got. No sloppy [message design] for me! I'm staying alert and in top condition. I'm not going to get caught [shooting from the hip, winging it, and then wondering why people don't respond] (1 Corinthians 9:24-27, *The Message*).

Message design always comes back to the receivers because the most important and eloquent message content becomes worthless if we fail to connect. Our cargo is too valuable to let it fail as a result of design and presentation errors. In addition to demographics, readiness, sophistication, and environment, we need to consider the audience's goals in relationship to our goals. Advertisers, seeking to target specific consumer groups, often create a "receiver constellation"—a graphic image depicting various representatives within the market. In the book *How to Change Your Church (Without Killing It)* (W Publishing Group, 2000), I apply this principle to determining who the church influencers are, how they are wired toward change in general, and their attitudes toward a specific idea or innovation. In this context, we'll use an audience constellation to analyze how various people are likely to receive the message.

Draw two concentric circles. The inner circle represents your primary target. These are the people you most want to connect with. The outer ring reflects your secondary target group—people who are apt to receive your message but who are not your primary focus. You should consider the potential impact of not connecting with these people, especially if they are influential resource givers or longtime members. The area outside the circle represents people who may receive the message but who are farthest from the target group. We'll call them peripheral eavesdroppers. At this point the pastoral nature suggests, "But I don't want to leave out anyone. I want everyone to be in the audience." The problem is, that isn't going to happen unless you are speaking to a very small and close-knit group.

PERIPHERAL
EAVESDROPPERS

A communicator has to know who may be left out of a specific message. Who did Jesus focus on in most of his messages? It was the disciples. He shared principles with them that others would not understand. The Sermon on the Mount was designed for his closest followers, even though many others eavesdropped. On the other hand, Jesus' public ministry tended to target the unchurched of his day while the scribes, Pharisees, and other religious leaders frequently eavesdropped. His approach to this group was significantly different from the others.

Not all audiences are alike. Some are very homogeneous (alike), and others are very heterogeneous (divergent). As the saying goes, "If you try to be all things to all people, you'll wind up being nothing to everybody." Churches need to determine their primary target group. For example, those that minister near Christian universities have to make difficult choices. They usually sit in the midst of at least three distinct ministry groups: students, faculty, and community. Many of these congregations cater to the faculty for a variety of reasons and then wonder why few students and local residents attend their services. Focusing on students means you run the risk of losing faculty members who are more educated, influential, and opinionated. Churches that target the unchurched in a local area run the risk of disconnecting with churched people, unless they provide other teaching venues, as well as periodically explain their strategy. Most churches choose to target Christians in their style of services and messages, thus alienating pre-Christians. (We'll discuss bridging this diversity gap in Chapter 10.)

So what do you do with people who are apt to be outside of a message's target group? Do you pretend they're not there and ignore them? If there is a clear distinction between circles, you may want to acknowledge the non-target people by explaining why you're taking the approach you are. For example, a wedding homily is usually designed for the bride and groom, but a simple sentence can connect the primary and secondary groups: "Janet and Steve, I want to talk to you about what the Bible says concerning God's definition of love, but the rest of us will be listening in so that we can improve our relationships as well." If you're primarily talking to seekers, you can bridge to the churched by saying, "I know many of you here have walked in faith for years, so you know by experience what I'm talking about. Your job is to not only make sure you don't take this for granted but also to share it with others."

Think of specific people who exist within these three constellation areas: primary target, secondary target, and peripheral eavesdroppers. Put a small circle in the appropriate area for each person or a representative of that person. If the person is already informed, inspired, or persuaded, depending on your message goal, place a plus sign in the circle. Leave the circle empty if the person is neutral or midrange. Place a minus symbol in the circle if the person is ignorant, uninspired, or adverse to the message. Some may say, "But I don't know where my audience is on this specific topic." If you want to create a message that truly connects, you'll need to do some investigation before you develop a constellation. In order to develop the skill, you'll want to physically do this a few times. After a while, it will likely become an intuitive discipline.

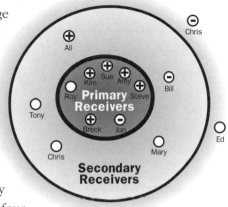

Now examine your constellation, using it to help answer key questions based on which of the four message types you are creating:

PERIPHERAL EAVESDROPPERS

Informative: What is the typical person like in this target zone? Is he interested in the topic? What is his IQ? Is she educated or uneducated? How old is he? How developed are her thinking processes? Does she have background in this area, or is this likely to be brand-new material? Do you need to establish any framework so the person has a way to handle the info? How do you know these things about the audience, and, therefore, how confident are you that you know this person? What do you want them to take away? What do you want them to do with this information after they leave?

Persuasive: How does the typical person in your target group feel about your topic? On a scale from 1 to 5 (1 = opposed cynic, 5 = adamant believer), how convinced is he of your theme? Are you starting in the hole, is this person neutral, or is he already sold? A realistic goal is to move him forward a notch or two, not more. What will it take to do that? Does she have emotional barriers or bad experiences that will need to be addressed before she can hear what you have to say? Will he consider you credible or not? What sort of attitude or action response will you want to see from this person after he or she leaves? How confident are you that you know this person?

Missional message creation means, "It's not about you!"

Inspirational: What is the emotional state of the individuals in this target group? What are they expecting when they receive the message? Are they damaged people or reasonably healthy? Will they be moved by the message's content, the medium used, or both? How do you know this? What stories are apt to connect with this group, and which will not? What are their backgrounds and shared interests? Are they young or old, rural or urban, simple or sophisticated, churched or unchurched, male or female? Do you have any way of measuring the effectiveness of this message? How confident are you that you know this audience?

Entertaining: What is the typical person in this target group? What would this person find entertaining, and why? What kind of entertainment has she pursued in the past? What are his age, cultural background, education, and income range? What form of entertainment might she find boring, offensive, or disengaging? (Sometimes you need to learn what to avoid as well as what to use.) How will you measure the effectiveness of this message? How confident are you that you know this target group?

"A windsock?
Are you all trying to tell me something?"

Message goal, content mass, time allotment, and audience constellation are vital components of creating effective messages. Understanding the relationship of these four primary design components gives you a foundation for understanding why specific messages do or do not connect.

⊐———— **Discussion/Thought Prompters** ————⊏

1. Review the last message you preached. How many info chunks did it have? Was it too heavy, too light, or just right?
2. What kind of messages do you prefer? How does your personal preference positively and negatively influence the way you go about designing your messages?
3. How do time constraints influence your message design? What would you do differently if you had more time or less time?
4. Of the four contextual factors, which do you think was most helpful to you?
5. Compare the adjacent audience constellation with the previous one in this chapter. If your goal was to inform, how would you approach each group differently, based on the target groups but also taking into account the secondary targets?

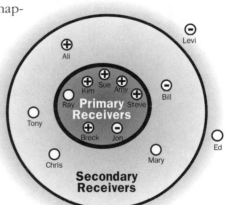

PERIPHERAL
EAVESDROPPERS

Chapter Five
Secret #5

Give Them Handles

"GRASP HERE"

T he next time you go on vacation, try carrying your luggage without using the handles. It's amazing how a u-shaped piece of plastic can help us so profoundly. Doors, lawnmowers, and coffee cups have handles. These grab bars make things usable. *Functionality* is the buzzword that won't go away, whether you're in the market for a copy machine, pair of shoes, or cell phone. Automobiles have comfortable seats and air conditioning, easy-to-read instrument panels, and CD players with digital displays. Office chair ads boast of their ergonomic design for hours of comfortable seating. Have you seen the latest model of the baby stroller? It has cup holders, a hand-held carrier that fits snuggly into the wheeled chassis, not to mention independently turning wheels and a cushioned handle that adjusts to a variety of heights. "In my day, we never had those fancy baby buggies." Life in the twenty-first century seems bent on catering to all aspects of our everyday lives to make them more convenient.

So what does this mean for us as communicators in the twenty-first century? How do we create and deliver messages in a way that connects with people, without whittling them down to something that God doesn't recognize?

Although I live a large portion of my life with my laptop computer, writing messages, articles, books, and e-mails, my use of the computer's potential is minimal. I have learned only enough to survive. I'd like to learn more, but the training manuals excite me about as much as getting a root canal. Occasionally a techie will sit down beside me and begin rambling off some cyber-babble, but I zone out after the first sentence—even though I sit patiently with a grin on my face, feigning interest. What I need is someone who'll show me how to better utilize my computer's capabilities based on how *I'll* use it, not on how some numbers cruncher or graphic artist will use it. I want someone who'll speak in simple English and demonstrate what pull-down menus to access and what icons I've overlooked. Then repeat it, allow me to write it down, or, better yet, let me practice. Otherwise I'll forget.

In terms of spirituality, pastors are theological techies trying to teach higher biblical principles to people who are immersed in other streams of living. Our audiences have little tolerance for Bible-babble, let alone Greek, Hebrew, or Aramaic. They want to know doctrine on an "as needed" basis. We pastors need to know theology, but if we understand it well enough, we should be able to translate it into everyday uses. People have not tried Christianity and found it lacking. They've lacked trying it because they can't unscrew the blasted lid or find the right pull-down menu. They don't know what buttons to push or what it looks like in their lives. They hear messages that sound intriguing but seem more applicable to monks or serial killers. On any given Sunday, scores of sermons are valiantly presented that never go anywhere for lack of handles that let people grasp them.

VELCRO POINTS

We've already mentioned that the secret ingredient to adult learning is relevance. Busy people are not interested in solutions for which they do not perceive problems. They want to know how it will help them cope with their lives and raise the quality of their families, work, and spirituality. But relevance is not the same as "application handles." Relevance will get you in the door, but as a communicator you don't want to merely be a messenger. You want to help the receivers install the message in their lives. So what can we do to make our messages stick, to help people take them home and use them?

Bridgeless messages tend to create segregated living so that our Christian lives fail to intersect with our school, work, community, and recreational lives.

Do not merely listen to the word, and so deceive yourselves. Do what it says. Anyone who listens to the word but does not do what it says is like a person who looks at his face in a mirror and, after looking at himself, goes away and immediately forgets what he looks like. But the man who looks intently into the perfect law that gives freedom, and continues to do this, not forgetting what he has heard, but doing it— he will be blessed in what he does (James 1:22-25).

Three questions are helpful in establishing Velcro points during design work:

1. How does this concept fit into everyday life?

This bridge-building skill is more difficult than you might think. Having lived in the Grand Canyon state, I know how deeply a river can cut into the crust of the earth. In communication, the cliff on one side of the river represents the everyday life of the receivers. The other side is the ageless truth that God wants us to know, both cognitively and experientially. No matter how masterfully you present the biblical principle, you cannot assume people know how to build a bridge across the river from a principle to their everyday lives.

Rick Warren wrote, "Growing up as a pastor's kid, I heard a lot of sermons at conferences and from my own father. As I listened, I'd find myself thinking, *This is good,* but in my Bible, next to the verses we were studying, I was constantly writing 'YBH'—Yes, but how? 'Be a Christlike father.' Yes, but how? 'Study the Bible.' Yes, but how?"[1] As our culture becomes increasingly secular, making the connection of God-truth with everyday life will be more difficult for our people.

2. What does this principle look like when it is implemented?

By their fruit you will recognize them. Do people pick grapes from thornbushes, or figs from thistles? Likewise every good tree bears good fruit, but a bad tree bears bad fruit. A good tree cannot bear bad fruit, and a bad tree cannot bear good fruit. Every tree that does not bear good fruit is cut down and thrown into the fire. Thus, by their fruit you will recognize them (Matthew 7:16-20).

What's the difference between a nice person who's a believer and a nice person who's an atheist? If Christian love looks different from human love, what is the difference? How does a person of faith respond to getting a pink slip at work as opposed to someone who either has no faith or who's not using it? The book of James is the model of twenty-first–century communication that connects because it links spiritual principles with everyday practices. Our job as communicators is to help our receivers discern what a life of faith looks like in their setting.

3. What are achievable steps toward implementing the truth?

When you buy a toy or piece of modular furniture that has those dreaded words *Some Assembly Required*, you expect to find instructions on how to put it together. Merely looking at a picture of the end result is insufficient for most of us. We need to see the various steps, what bolt goes into what piece, and the correct sequence for assembly. "As the body without the spirit is dead, so faith without deeds is dead" (James 2:26).

APPLICATION MINUS LEGALISM

Although we're all looking for handles so we can be more fruitful, there are potential dangers. Connecting biblical truths with behavioral applications has pros and cons that communicators need to confront early in their message creation. The human tendency is to wear our faith inside out, so that the fruit of our faith—Christlike behavior—precedes the root. This mind-set has been called a variety of things such as legalism, Pharisee-ism, and works theology.

The goal is to illustrate what the gospel looks like in everyday attitudes and behaviors, without reducing it to the constrictions of a cookbook. Some people seek behavioral approaches to implementing Christianity, while others reject them. A message creator should keep in mind the potential benefits and liabilities of using practical ideas (handles).

Benefits of Practical Suggestions
- They give people ideas they can apply in their situations.
- They provide ways to quantify spiritual growth, which tends to be intangible and difficult to measure.

- They help the communicators think in terms of relevance and living godly lives in a secular world.
- They endear people to the gospel as they see an ageless truth in a contemporary context.

Limitations of Practical Suggestions
- They can give the impression of salvation by works and legalism.
- They can alienate those who may not relate to the application example.
- They can compromise a truth by reducing it to a matter of specific behaviors.
- They can be controversial if people focus on the application instead of the principle behind it.
- They can distort a doctrine by suggesting a behavior it doesn't really support.

Biblical Examples of Practically Applying Faith
- Jesus' command for his followers to wash feet (John 13)
- Abraham called to sacrifice Isaac (Genesis 22)
- The Ten Commandments (Exodus 20)
- Jonah commanded to go to Nineveh (Jonah 1)
- Jesus' direction for the wealthy man to sell his possessions and give them to the poor (Luke 18:22)

There are hundreds of biblical examples of faith sprouting feet. Granted, some of these examples are direct commands of God rather than applications of a message, but the themes are enduring. Most of us are pretty good at displaying the biblical principle in the church showroom, but an effective communicator helps the congregant see what it looks like in his or her home and office. If you can get your receivers to sample the concept, to test-drive it for a few days, you significantly increase the likelihood that it will have the opportunity to transform their lives.

A friend of mine, Denny Bellesi, garnered national attention when his parishioners were given various amounts of money after a message on giving. They were each to use it in the life of another person and report their experiences. Since then, scores of other churches have experimented with versions of this idea. Another friend, Steve Sjogren, continually provides an array of service-evangelism ideas to his congregation, from cleaning gas station restrooms to handing out free water at parades. The ideas for implementing message principles are limited only by our imaginations. Brainstorm applications with a team of creative friends and staff members.

The challenge with broadly cast application ideas is that accountability becomes difficult. Unless receivers are in a small group that specifically focuses on applying these ideas, measuring results is difficult for most congregations. Your job as a message designer is to put handles on the concepts you teach, in order to help receivers connect with them. Here are three ideas for making this happen:

1. Message Illustrations

The rule of thumb is that each concept (info chunk) should be illustrated. That way you tap both the left-brain hemisphere (intellect) and right-brain hemisphere (emotion). This is the Greek philosophy of public speaking: *logos* (logic) + *pathos* (emotion) + *ethos* (speaker credibility) = good communication. The illustrations in your message provide handles on how people can put into practice the principle that you've unpacked. Intentionally craft application illustrations that demonstrate your point in an everyday situation. And don't always give the polished version; you may tell stories of failed attempts or application struggles. Getting people to see themselves through the eyes of others is also helpful because most of us are more frustrated by a lack of godliness in others than in ourselves. Lean toward simple, everyday stories rather than sensational, bigger-than-life illustrations. Here's an example.

"This week, I was late for a meeting, and I was stuck in traffic following a blue-haired snowbird with Minnesota plates. As the car made its slow turn at the intersection, I got stopped by the red light and had to wait another two minutes before I could turn. As I sat there, I thought, 'Why am I always in a rush? What's so important about my agenda that I let it ruin my attitude and mess with my ability to get along with others?' I began to realize that patience is not just something to strive for; it's a byproduct of pursuing a centered life that has God as the axle."

2. Testimonials

Have you ever gone to someone else's house and picked up décor ideas that you could use in your own home? Sometimes we learn how to implement a spiritual concept from the life of another person. The strategic use of a testimonial is a means of getting the attention off you. "Well, of course we expect *you* to apply this principle; you're the pastor." By telling someone else's story (with permission), doing a live interview, or videotaping the person, you can show this principle via a peer pilgrim.

For example, during a series on Philemon, we discussed the concept of forgiveness, since Paul was exhorting Philemon to accept his runaway slave, Onesimus. I invited a woman whose former husband had slept with her sister and sister-in-law to join me on the platform. Because we'd rehearsed beforehand, we were able to highlight elements of her story in less than five minutes, but it made a big impact. Her testimony became a handle for people to see how the ancient principle of forgiveness might look in their situations, through the experience of another person who'd been betrayed.

In a Christmas miniseries on gift giving, I interviewed a woman in our church who had just donated bone marrow. The recipient was an eleven-year-old girl with cancer who was a complete stranger. This woman's act of kindness was a powerful illustration of living out God's grace to us through tangible means.

3. After-Message Mints

Nearly every Sunday, the message outline on the handout ends with application ideas to increase the residual effect. These are akin to discussion questions you might find in a small group Bible study guide, but they are designed for personal reflection. Some of them are contemplative in nature, while others are quite behavioral.

Here are a few examples:

After a message on hope:

What hope-busters are you wrestling with now?

What is one area in which you're struggling to persevere?

List three mini-victories (blessings) in your life today.

After a message about pride:

List three areas that suggest pride/self-will in your life right now.

Write a note to a friend, admitting a failure, mistake, or oversight on your part.

Call or e-mail a peer to affirm his or her accomplishment.

After a message on the temptation to compromise:

On a scale from 1 to 5 (1 low, 5 high)…

_____ People around me can tell a difference because Christ is in my life.

_____ I modify my standards when I'm with people who do not share my faith.

List one area in which you're tempted to compromise, and consider telling a friend for accountability.

By providing handles with your messages, you increase the likelihood that your message will be listened to and carried away for enduring impact.

"… listening to the announcements … call me back during the sermon … "

Discussion/Thought Prompters

1. What is your biggest challenge in coming up with appropriate message handles?
2. Review a recent message or two that you've preached, and note any handles. How could you have improved or increased them?
3. What was the most helpful idea you gleaned from this chapter?
4. What's your view on the limitations/dangers of the overuse of applications?
5. What kind of handles can you create in this week's message?

Chapter Six
Secret #6

Bait the
Hook

THE MOST IMPORTANT THREE MINUTES OF ANY TALK

We did a two-week series on John the Baptist. John was a bit quirky (camel skins, locusts, wilderness…need I say more?), so we thought that "Born to Be Wild" might be an appropriate series title. We wanted those who felt they had a wild streak in them to understand that many of God's people did not reside in a "classic Christian" box and that God can use their free spirit, if they let him. The first week, we played the song "Born to Be Wild" as we showed a video clip of motorcycles from *Easy Rider*. The next week, we had some motorcycles parked on the patio as people arrived. Then, in the opening, we interviewed one of our members who had recently attended the giant biker rally in Sturgis, South Dakota. Just before the message, "Born to Be Wild" started playing and the motorcycle video came on the screens again, but then the outside doors of the auditorium opened, and I drove in on a Harley, wearing a leather vest, head scarf, and fingerless gloves. The people roared and then applauded. "Now that I have your attention…"

"A Russian proverb offers wise counsel to the preacher: 'It is the same with men as with donkeys: whoever would hold them fast must get a very good grip on their ears!'"
—HADDON ROBINSON[1]

A lot of people come to church expecting to be

bored so they're not disappointed by the time they leave. But if you want to connect with today's audiences, you need to be able to get and maintain their attention. Adrenaline fiends, accustomed to sound bites and fast-track living, have a difficult time giving prolonged attention to low-energy communication. The most important part of any talk is the first three minutes. You have about three minutes to convince people to listen to the rest of your talk. Gaining attention from the start does not mean you'll hold them for the duration. (We'll talk about that in the next secret.) But if you don't catch them early, fat chance you'll connect with them down the road.

Harry Beckwith, in his bestselling book on marketing, *Selling the Invisible*, described today's fast-paced culture: "People with little time—almost all people today—are more apt to make first impressions as snap judgments, and then base all their later decisions on them. The smart marketer must be aware of this strong tendency. First impressions have never been more critical—they take hold very quickly, and they become the anchors to which you and your success are tied."[2] What applies to marketers applies to communicators.

So how do you bait the hook early on so receivers will engage with you? Here are a variety of ideas you can use. Any one approach used continually will likely fail, but keeping things changing is a great way to play on the curiosity factor: "I wonder what's going to happen today. I love the openers." Interest is inversely proportional to predictability.

Jokes: *The Tonight Show's* opening, comedic monologue is a proven method of engaging people in what is otherwise an ordinary talk show. An opening joke can work just as well for you, if done well. Rehearse the joke so that it flows. If you don't have a natural sense of humor, run it by someone who does to make sure it doesn't fall flat. The only thing worse than no jokes is consistently bad jokes. You know your personality. A very few people just can't do humor well and shouldn't try. But most of us benefit by telling a personal story, Internet anecdote, or joke. The power of humor at the start of a message is that it allows you to build rapport with receivers. It's not about the content of the

> *"Writers refer to the first few sentences as the lead. The lead is the most critical part of an article: if it fails to hook readers, they turn the page."*
> —MARK GALLI AND CRAIG BRIAN LARSON[3]

story as much as it is about the relationship you want to build. You want to endear yourself to the receivers so they'll be more apt to listen to what you say next. When a joke has little to do with the message, you need to move quickly to the content, but it's a great initial attention-grabber.

> *Don't try to solve problems with skits. Leave the receivers wanting more, setting up the role of God's Word for solving the issue the skit raised.*

Drama skit: For centuries, the arts have been pretty much lost by the church. But the church is beginning to embrace the visual arts, dance, and drama. Live theater is an entertaining way to engage people. The vehicle is drama, but the skit can set up a problem, illustrate an everyday situation, or bring a comedic look at ourselves. Reader's theater, humor, tragedy, and drama are all styles of short sketches that draw people into the topic.

Message creators should consider the role of a drama. Putting a skit into the service schedule just because some "happening" church is doing it doesn't make sense. Again, no acting is better than consistently bad acting. There must be a level of excellence; otherwise, the audience will feel anxious for the performers, and the cumulative result will be more negative than positive. Make sure the sketch relates to the topic of the day. Most skits you purchase from other churches will need to be edited to fit the talent you have and the specific angle you're taking with a message. You can rarely import someone else's skit unchanged if you want to be effective.

Movie clip: By using a license (see www.mplc.com for information), churches can legally access the work of multimillion-dollar budgets that produce powerful media presentations with some of the finest actors in the world. With so many movies in DVD format, finding an exact clip is easier than ever, since you can click to movie segments instead of pushing "fast forward" and "rewind" to locate a section of videotape.

There are a growing number of resources that give you themes of potential movie clips (for example, www.hollywoodjesus.com and www.ministryandmedia.com). Be aware that these sources can become dated and you'll have to search for something that fits the angle of your message. Another challenge is making sure the clip is fitting for church use—minus sex, drugs, violence, and profanity. Most people have higher moral standards for media within their churches than they do in their homes or local theaters. Some churches are sensitive to the idea that using a clip is an unspoken endorsement of the movie, which may be far from Christian. Knowing your ministry context is the key. The power of an appropriate movie clip is that it is stimulating and engaging, is often familiar to many in your audience, and provides a contemporary link to age-old truths. Besides, it's a great excuse to go to the movies in order to "do sermon research."

Video graphic: Besides using clips from movies, there is a growing number of short media presentations that provide the sizzle that engages interest. The problem with providing a list of current resources is that they can quickly become outdated. By accessing ministry resources such as Rev. magazine and www.emergingminister.com, as well as churches that use media, you can find out what's available. A computer-based presentation program, graphic roll-ins, and other media presentations grab attention early in order to engage the audience. As the price of video-production equipment and software decreases and the number of people who are familiar with video production increases, more local churches can create their own media. This also allows you to personalize media for your local congregation and specific message theme.

Story: Good storytellers are always popular. People as diverse as Jesus, Abraham Lincoln, and Mark Twain are renowned for using stories to communicate truth. You can see the power of a story as you observe the audience's eye contact. When concepts are communicated, people often look down at notes, peer around at others, or gaze into the distance. But when a story begins, people look up to focus their attention. The reason is that most people are visual learners. They find it easier and more interesting to create mental pictures from stories than from concepts. The mistake many speakers make is that they fail to link the story to a message theme or to draw a conclusion that hooks the receivers. Listeners think, "Cute story, but what in the world did that have to do with anything?"

Dramatic entrance: Although many pastoral types may not feel comfortable using this tool, a dramatic entrance (such as riding in on a motorcycle) is a powerful way to attract attention at the start. Here are a few dramatic entrances we've used in the past that may stimulate your creativity:

• Message on emotional baggage from the past: Wear a large backpack throughout the message, and then take it off at the end to signify forgiveness and letting go.

• Message on death, the hereafter: Pallbearers bring an empty casket down the aisle as organ music plays quietly.

• Message on caring for the helpless: Dress like a homeless person, and enter from the back, pushing a grocery cart with bags.

• Message on "climbing the ladder" in pursuit of success: Give your talk while standing on the rungs of a stepladder, moving up a rung with each point. *[Editor's Note: Group Publishing is not responsible for pastors falling off ladders!]*

• Message on spiritual cripples: Walk in on crutches, and deliver the message while using a crutch to illustrate each point.

• Message on living the Spirit-filled life: Play a *Superman* movie clip as the pastor enters from the back of the auditorium, wearing a Superman costume on which the S signifies the Spirit.

• Messages that benefit from getting audience feedback on a topic: Begin with the pastor sitting in the crowd, using a roving microphone to talk to people.

Song: Music always carries some message, but when used strategically, it can set up a sermon by engaging the audience in the process. An appropriate song after a drama can be a double attention-grabber: mood setter and point maker. Christian songs are often good ways to conclude a message because they tend to focus on solutions. A way to begin a message is with a Christian song that adequately establishes the problem or, better yet, a secular song that depicts a life situation, social values, or an issue that begs for a biblical response. Here are a few classic rock/jazz examples:

• A message on money can begin with The Grateful Dead's hit "Money Money" or the Beatles' "Can't Buy Me Love."

BMI, the organization that manages copyrights of secular music, has said that church services do not qualify as "public performances" and, thus, no license or payment is required.

The nitroglycerin of public speaking is intensity. *The formula is Intensity = Urgency + Importance x Speaker Passion.*

- A message on contentment can begin with The Rolling Stones' "Satisfaction (I Can't Get No)."
- A message on Ecclesiastes 3 can begin with The Byrds' "Turn! Turn! Turn! (To Everything There Is a Season)."
- A message series on Jude can begin with an intro from "Hey Jude" by the Beatles.
- A message on priority or time can begin with The Doobie Brothers' "Minute By Minute."
- A message on community can begin with Sister Sledge's "We Are Family."

It's best to do these songs live, but you obviously need to make sure you have the musical talent to pull it off. The shock factor of hearing a popular, secular tune in church is enough to engage people by itself, but it doesn't truly work unless you make the tie-in to the message of the day. Sometimes you can just use sound bites as people enter, during fellowship time, or as a transition between parts of the service. The subliminal impact is often sufficient to build intrigue.

Intensity: The best message-creation efforts will not reach their potential if the message is not presented in a manner that emotionally engages receivers. The single most important element that transforms good speaking into great communication is intensity. Message intensity elevates the perceived value of a topic. Now more than ever, when our society is barraged by an incessant flow of unsolicited messages, the ones that will get noticed are those that have intensity. Our messages must stand out in the crowd. They need to compel listeners to pay attention to them, to heed their call.

> Several years ago, representatives of seven famous investment banking firms flew into Seattle, Washington, to pitch Starbucks. Each firm made its pitch and impressed the audience so much that CEO Howard Schultz later reported that he couldn't tell the seven firms apart—except for one tiny thing.
> "Commitment and passion. That was the difference," Schultz told Fortune magazine in 1997.[4]

Most effective communicators are intense, though this element tends to be somewhat intangible. It looks different from person to person, but the feel is the same. "Listen to me! What I'm telling you is important! It's urgent that you hear and understand what I'm going to say!" There are a variety of nonverbal elements that make up intensity. For some it rests more in the eyes. For others it's a serious demeanor that conveys the feeling of emergency. Boldness of gestures and gait, loudness of voice, and a look of sincerity are all vehicles for communicating intensity. Mother Teresa, Billy Graham, and Martin Luther King Jr. had different styles, but all had intensity in their communication. The intensity factor of any message can make or break its connectivity.

You can be intense and still smile, laugh, use humor, and act like you're enjoying yourself. But you can't give the impression that your message is not a big deal. "Hey, this is what the Bible says. You can take it or leave it. It'll help your life if you choose to believe it, but if you don't, life will go on without it." This kind of lackluster attitude will diminish the impact of your message, no matter how well you've designed it.

URGENT AND IMPORTANT

Intensity addresses two vital questions: "How important is this?" and "How urgent is it?" The first question has to do with the potential benefits if I understand what is being communicated and the detriment or dangers if I do not. The latter question has to do with the timeliness of the message. Is time of the essence, or can this wait? Stephen Covey talks about the relationship of urgency and importance in his book *The Seven Habits of Highly Effective People.*[5]

Take a look at the chart on the following page. Quadrant IV items are of low urgency and low importance. Most of the messages with which we're bombarded every day, from advertisements to trivial factoids, fall into this category. Our mental screens get clogged with these spamlike messages, sometimes causing us to miss more important ones due to information overload. Quadrant III messages are the result of shrewd marketing ploys and noisemakers that grab our attention but

> *"There are three types of preachers: those to whom you cannot listen; those to whom you can listen; and those to whom you must listen."*
>
> —HADDON ROBINSON[6]

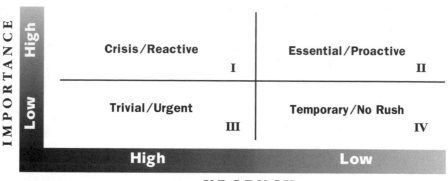

result in little long-term gain. The tyranny of the urgent is the theme of this sector, resulting in tail-chasing activities that leave us weary but with little to show for it at the end of the day, year, or life. Legitimate crises make up Quadrant I, resulting in life/job/family-threatening events that, if left unattended, will significantly lower or end our quality of life. People are most responsive to Quadrants III and I because of their urgency—sometimes regardless of their importance.

The most challenging issues in life tend to come in Quadrant II, for they are important but lack perceived urgency. We can get away with putting them on the back burner. They do not scream for our attention. Unfortunately, this is generally the ministry realm we face as preachers. The gospel we propagate has eternal benefits and dangers, but the lack of perceived urgency hinders our ability to naturally increase the intensity of our messages.

Foxhole spirituality is proof that combined urgency and importance are strong motivators. But when we believe we have plenty of time, we tend to defer decisions. It is human tendency to procrastinate and overestimate the number of our days. Part of our job as prophetic messengers is to constantly remind people that our time is shorter than we think—without coming across as pessimistic "doomsdayers."

> Here's what I'll do: I'll tear down my barns and build bigger ones. Then I'll gather in all my grain and goods, and I'll say to myself, "Self, you've done well! You've got it made and can now retire. Take it easy and have the time of your life!"
>
> Just then God showed up and said, "Fool! Tonight you die. And

your barnful of goods—who gets it?" (Luke 12:18-20, *The Message*).

Show me, O Lord, my life's end and the number of my days; let me know how fleeting is my life. You have made my days a mere hand-breadth; the span of my years is as nothing before you. Each man's life is but a breath (Psalm 39:4-5).

Why, you do not even know what will happen tomorrow. What is your life? You are a mist that appears for a little while and then vanishes (James 4:14).

Think of the emotional ploys of the evangelist who tries to raise the sense of urgency. He points to a seat in the church and says, "Last week, the man who sat where you're sitting left the service without making a commitment to God, and he was hit by a train on his way home." *A Thief in the Night* and similar movies gained huge numbers of responders by creating such a sense of urgency that, if people did not decide for Christ before going home, they felt they'd be lost to eternal damnation. Right or wrong, today's crowd is either more cynical or more savvy. The ability to elevate urgency is becoming more difficult as a competing voices suggest that their messages are the most urgent.

The job of the communicator who desires to connect is to raise the level of perceived importance as well as the degree of urgency. Itinerant communicators have an easier job at this—they are here today and gone tomorrow. Prophets usually conveyed a greater sense of intensity because of this. Priestly, pastoral messengers are more challenged because if everything is urgent, then nothing is. If we cry "wolf" too often, people begin to dismiss our messages as hype and hoopla. A shrewd communicator should play the urgent card strategically, while consciously discerning how to elevate both importance and urgency on a regular basis.

A sender can raise the level of urgency/importance by addressing some of the following questions during the message-creation process:

- What is the danger of not buying into this idea?
- What are the real benefits of believing this idea?
- Why is time of the essence?
- What will I lose by not acting quickly?
- What will I gain by responding right away?
- On a scale of 1 to 5, how much will this matter in the next five years?
- On a scale of 1 to 5, how much will this matter for eternity?

ENTHUSIASM IS CONTAGIOUS

Another intensity element is the excitement of the communicator. You reap what you sow. Preachers use this to motivate their audiences, but it's true of us, too: If you catch on fire, people will come to watch you burn.

The old story is told of a well-known atheist who was seen attending a John Wesley service. An onlooker challenged the man: "I thought you didn't believe in God."

"I don't," he responded, "But John Wesley sure does."

We've preached it a number of times: *Enthusiasm* literally means *entheos*—in God, God in me. You can say "fire" in public, but it's illegal to say it with enthusiasm unless something's burning. People are emotional beings. We are influenced by the emotions of those around us. When people display excitement, energy, and boldness, it rubs off. Passion that stays locked inside fails to help messages connect. Let it out!

When I was a freshman in college, I was running from a call to ministry. I enrolled in classes to become an architect. I took a physics class at Iowa State University, which was one of the most interesting courses I've ever taken (even though I only got a C). I remember it because the professor was a short, wiry man who loved his subject. He'd illustrate formulas and laws of physics with a variety of interesting experiments. At times he'd stand on top of the lab table to perform a demonstration. He'd laugh, shout, gesture boldly, and engross the large class of college freshmen like few other professors I've met. As the saying goes, "There are no boring subjects, just boring teachers." Savvy students take a course because of who teaches it rather than what the class catalog says about it.

Listen to Joel Osteen, Ken Blanchard, Bill Hybels, Tony Robbins, or John Maxwell, and you know they have what old-timers called "fire in the belly." They believe in what they are talking about (or at least they give the impression they do). Cerebral communicators can impress us with knowledge, but the world is not moved by mere mental endeavors. Passion drives free will. Head matters are rarely enough to ignite our hearts. Receivers want to know, "Does the speaker believe what he's saying? How much does he believe it? Is he willing to sacrifice other things for what he's teaching?" Passion drives vision. If there is a single ingredient that will significantly improve the presentation of nearly any message, it is the elevation of passion. Either become passionate about the things you talk about or talk about your passions. Dispassionate preaching yields few results for the senders or receivers.

THE ANOINTING

As a collegian studying for the ministry, I had an opportunity to speak at Kansas City Youth for Christ, a very exciting Saturday evening rally that was televised in the metro area. Al Metsker had led this local group into one of the largest branches of Youth for Christ in the nation. He invited dynamic young preachers to speak to the youth during the rallies. I'd been on the program a couple of times as a ventriloquist, but then they asked me to speak. I was thrilled!

Unfortunately, it didn't work as well as I'd hoped. Granted, I lacked experience and had never spoken before so many people, but I failed primarily because I hadn't sufficiently prepared myself spiritually. My words were right, but I spoke without the power of God in my life. They never invited me back. Since then, I've learned more and more to recognize when I'm out of it spiritually. People may still come up and provide a token compliment or word of encouragement, but even the best-designed speech isn't what it could be without the anointing of God's Spirit on it.

We cannot discuss effective message creation in the context of ministry without addressing the importance of spiritual power in the life of the sender. Message design is never a substitute for prayerful preparation, but neither is spiritual pursuit an excuse for haphazard sermon work. Some pastors are under the impression that all they have to do is seek God and he'll make up the difference for mediocre message preparation. In high school, I attended a church where the pastor occasionally would skip his Sunday evening message. Our theory was that when he'd done a shoddy job preparing the evening sermon, the Spirit would conveniently show up in worship, prayer, and testimonies, so he'd run out of time to speak. But it isn't a choice between either good message prep or spiritual anointing; you need both/and. We need to both work on message-design matters and make sure we're humbling ourselves before

"If God's not in it, what's the use anyway?"

—JOHN 15:5 (AUTHOR'S PARAPHRASE)

God in order to seek his blessing and anointing.

There is a mystical element to what we do as preachers. We are conduits through which God's Spirit flows. When we merely present a cleverly contrived message that we've produced in our study, we've failed to do what God desires. He wants us to know his heart, to create a message that truly conveys his concerns for his people. It's not about us; it's about him. Getting out of the way may be the most difficult task that most of us face as communicators of God's truth. The burden is heavy, the responsibility awesome. The common trap is to write the message and then pray for God's blessing on it. This after-the-fact approach is akin to the way we nonchalantly go about saying grace prior to eating. A Jewish friend of mine joked about the Christian tradition of saying the blessing before each meal. He said, "We just seek God's blessing on the groceries as we unload them and that takes care of it, all at one time." Perhaps the right process is praying before, during, and after preparation.

To be a master communicator, a purveyor of godly truth, you cannot accomplish what you must without the touch of God on your message. Paul wrote, "My message and my preaching were not with wise and persuasive words, but with a demonstration of the Spirit's power, so that your faith might not rest on men's wisdom, but on God's power" (1 Corinthians 2:4-5).

Jim Cymbala wrote, "If a church is only methodology and organizational technique and clever advertising, it is departing from what God planned it to be. There should always be the element of the supernatural assistance."[7]

E.M. Bounds wrote, "The power of Christ's dispensation is a fiery pulpit—not a learned pulpit, not a popular pulpit, not an eloquent pulpit, but a pulpit on fire with the Holy Ghost."[8]

Unfortunately, preaching is more difficult than writing a clever speech. Paying the price in message preparation is a matter not only of research and strategic design but also of spiritual wrestling. God gave Jacob the moniker Israel—literally "God wrestler"—which became the name of an entire nation of people who were called to exhibit God's power and presence to the world.

Prayer and fasting (as opposed to fast praying) are keys to making a good God connection. The pursuit of a holy life, confessing known and unknown transgressions, maintaining loving relationships, and living in obedience to God are proven vehicles for increasing the flow of the Holy Spirit in our lives. Spirit-led messengers always supersede those conveying the exact same messages without the anointing. While we cannot manipulate God or coerce his movement in our communication, we are certainly responsible for intentionally seeking the touch of God in our lives. If your messages are not what you want them to be, even after much effort, you may need to focus on the spiritual dimension of your preaching. The touch of the Spirit on your words and presentation is a powerful thing that transcends human explanation or understanding. The Spirit brings a freedom for boldness unlike any human effort. "Thus saith the Lord" commands the attention of people to repentance…and occasionally toward stoning. Consider both the potential rewards and risks.

LETTING GO

Studies reveal that the number one human fear is of public speaking. (Based on that, pastors should get hazard pay.) People are afraid they'll say or do something by which others will judge them negatively. But ministerial presentation is not about you; it's about God and them. Self-consciousness and concern about how you're doing interfere with your ability to let go. Don't hold back. You've been preparing all week for this moment. Reservations within the communicator inhibit receptivity. Audiences love it when a speaker is into the message. Reckless abandon is an important part of enhancing intensity. When you're holding back for whatever reason, it's like driving with the parking brake engaged.

Letting go is not only about loosening up as a speaker. It also means letting go spiritually so that you are free from the fears of (1) what others are thinking about you or (2) failing to get your point across. This is not a matter of irresponsibility or failing to care. Rather, it's a matter of losing yourself in the midst of God. When the anointing of God is on your life and your message, you have an energy that includes confidence, intensity, and a supernatural ability to speak directly to the hearts

Getting up to speak is like bungee jumping; do your homework and then go for it.

of the people who receive the message.

A good opening, use of the arts, intensity, urgency, enthusiasm, and the anointing are key elements in getting people to bite the hook on your message. They should be apparent within the first few moments of a presentation.

The post-sermon interview.

Used by artist's permission. Reprinted from Leadership Journal.

Discussion/Thought Prompters

1. Who do you know who baits the hook well and engages his or her audience early on in his or her speeches?
2. Review a recent sermon/talk you've given. What did you do well to bait the hook? What could you have done more effectively?
3. Think about an intense communicator who engages you with his or her speaking.
4. What can you do to elevate the urgency and importance of your next talk without exaggerating it to the point of losing credibility?
5. How would you rate the spiritual intensity of your speaking ministry on a scale of 1 to 5? How can you increase the touch of God in your life?

Chapter Seven

Secret #7

Avoid the Bore-Snore Factor

LET ME ENTERTAIN YOU!

While attending a leadership development think tank, one megachurch senior pastor stood and wearily said, "I hope my kids don't go into the ministry. I'm sick and tired of entertaining our people. It's a relentless job." Most of us who've been a part of churches reaching pre-Christians understand that frustration. Boomers are consumers, and, well, busters aren't much different. But if you want to be a communicator who connects in the twenty-first century, you must be an entertainer in the literal sense of the word.

To *entertain* literally means "to hold in tension." Most Sunday messages are entertainment-deprived in that they fail to hold the attention (at-tension) of the listeners. I grew up on a farm, and we were frequently towing or pulling a vehicle out of a ditch. We'd hook a chain or towrope from the hitch to the bumper. Dad would do the pulling, and I'd be in the towed vehicle. He'd warn me, "Make sure you keep the chain tight." Otherwise it was liable to be yanked and break. The same is true in communication. If you allow too much emotional slack between you and your receivers, a disconnect is apt to happen. Church health guru Lyle Schaller said, "Today consumers have an entertainment orientation, and whether we like it or not, pastors must acknowledge the influence of those expectations."[1]

CHARTING THE ENERGY LEVEL OF A MESSAGE

Have you ever noticed that some days you feel energetic and upbeat, whereas you seem lethargic and pensive on others? Some people call these biorhythms. Thanks to modern technology, we can visually measure patterns, beats, and rhythms, whether they are of a voice, a heartbeat, or a radio frequency. Imagine an instrument that could measure the energy flow of a worship service or message. The printout might look like this:

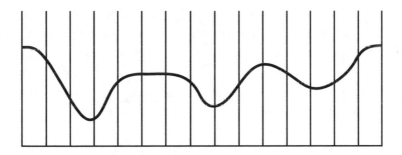

Every message has a pattern—moments when high energy results in heightened awareness, and periods when there is a lull or rest. As the preacher talks, the energy is ebbing and flowing. All parts of the message are not created equal, nor should they be. The goal of messages that connect is to create a healthy energy pattern in which intentional moments of added tension are followed by elements of tension relief. When reeling in a big fish, the angler must pull back and then let go, pull back and let go, or else he's apt to lose his prize. Messages that do not connect usually fail to create sufficient tension when it is needed and/or allow too much time where energy has ebbed and people begin wandering. Just as the eye is drawn to light, the hearts and minds of your receivers react to energy, whether it comes from a crying baby, a video clip, someone getting up to go to the restroom, or an animated illustration.

Communication tension is akin to flexing a muscle. You can only push a muscle so far until it tires. After doing a set of repetitions, a weight trainer will rest the muscle before doing another set. A similar rhythm is important in communication. The parts creating tension tend to be the stuff that conveys the most content. Talking about concepts causes mental strain. The audience is thinking about what you're saying.

> *Never confuse your talking with their listening.*

Too much of this, uninterrupted, results in brain fatigue and feeling overwhelmed, so the mind seeks relief. Gifted communicators discern energy ebb and flow intuitively. They sense that the audience has bitten off all it can and needs to swallow, relax, and exhale. So smart communicators crack a joke, change their posture, tell an engrossing story, or even do something that doesn't seem to fit the theme of the message but is an intentional tactic to relieve tension.

Elementary school teachers know that if they assign only concentrated, classroom, sit-at-the-desk work, kids will learn only so much. Work periods need to be interrupted with recess, lunch, naps, crafts, and other activities for maximum learning to take place. Communicators cannot drone on and on about a Bible passage or scriptural principle and assume that their people are getting it. Good message creators anticipate the message's energy level in order to intentionally raise and lower audience engagement to maximize effectiveness.

The optimum message energy pattern is similar to the one graphed here. A typical Sunday morning message should have three or four crests and troughs. A speaker begins with an engaging introduction in order to

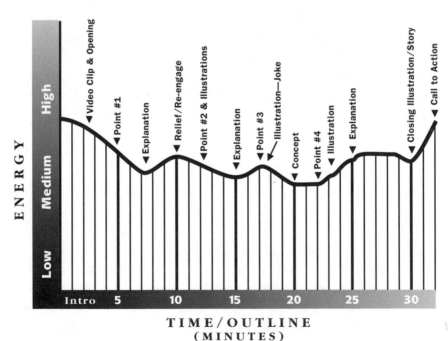

TIME/OUTLINE
(MINUTES)

"sell" the audience on listening further. The first main point should be the second strongest point. Again, you're still partially in the selling mode, in that you want to engage listeners and let them know this will be worth their while. It's equivalent to the first bite of the entree. Pack your less exciting points within the body of the message. The strongest point should be your last one. By this time, people have traveled a journey with you. Make it worth their while by rewarding them with a good finale. Dessert comes at the end of the meal.

You say, "Well, what if the strongest point doesn't come last in the text?" Then skip it in the natural sequence and come back to it. Too many pastors end their messages on weak points, creating anticlimactic finales. Even Christian funerals deserve a good finish. End with a zinger, the point that will make people scratch their heads and awaken their souls as they leave the service.

CREATING TENSION

Tension, in this context, has to do with stress that is created when a concept or topic requires people to think, to process. The equivalent is when you're driving a car that's pulling a trailer, and you start up a hill. Perhaps you're confronting a behavior or value with a more biblical one. You may be discussing the historical or cultural background. In general, talk that is related to an info chunk, even if it is illustrative, tends to be tension-building. Unless the story is whimsical or comedic, it is likely creating more tension than it is relieving because you're taxing the audience. Reading a portion of Scripture, introducing a main point, and supporting it with subpoints are generally tension creators. Your goal is to get people seriously thinking about the claims of the Scripture and how they apply to their lives.

You can create positive tension with vocal variety, such as speaking more loudly or softly and fluctuating emphases. Gesturing with your arms, hands, and face and other physical animation are nonverbal means of engaging attention. People tend to focus on movement more than stationary items. They are more likely to lose interest when a speaker speaks in a monotone and stays behind a large pulpit. Aimless pacing is not the solution, but specific movement helps. Our senses are such that they tend to shut down when there is no new stimulus to keep them activated. Consider them to be a motion detector that shuts off the light when there is no movement and turns on with action.

Creating points of tension is crucial because this is where receivers are most apt to connect with the content of your message. This is the gem in the setting that you've worked to prepare. You want them to be inspired, to understand, or to be persuaded, depending on the goal of your message. But these processes can drain energy by creating stress among the receivers. Too much of a good thing becomes a bad thing. The car pulling the trailer uphill will find its engine flagging and over-heating. People will begin to check out as if you'd never created tension. They'll start looking around, daydreaming, doodling on their handouts, whispering to their spouses, or watching the interesting person sitting two rows in front on the side. Most speakers fail to recognize when a majority of people have surpassed their energy limit, or at least do not know what to do when they realize it. They need to relieve the tension, which re-engages people and raises the energy level.

MULTISENSORY SERVICES

One way to raise energy or relieve tension is to intentionally engage multiple senses. This is an element of message complexity that we discussed previously. Musical interludes, background ambience, visual aids, and media graphics are the most common forms of multisensory stimulation. Jesus did this often by pointing out surroundings as he spoke (fish, sheep, vineyards). During the Last Supper alone, there were smell and taste (Passover meal, wine, bread) and touch (washing feet).

Touch: Provide something for people to hold during the message or touch at some point during or after the service.
- Hand out palm branches on Palm Sunday.
- Staple a piece of sandpaper and a swatch of satin to the handout to illustrate two ways your demeanor affects others.
- Distribute large nails when you talk about the Crucifixion.
- Turn on large fans, blowing across the congregation, to illustrate how the Holy Spirit is a wind that blows through our lives, invisible but present.

• Revelation discusses churches being hot, cold, and lukewarm. Provide Crock-Pots of hot, cold, and lukewarm water for people to touch.

Smell: One of our most powerful senses is our olfactory system, which can also be a memorable ministry tool with some thought and creative preparation.

• When discussing brokenness in the context of how God uses difficult things to fertilize our souls, bring in pails of manure to make your point.

• If you talk about Jesus being the bread of life or asking God for your daily bread, have bread ovens cooking bread around the perimeter of the sanctuary so people smell it as they enter.

• When talking about prayer, have aromatic candles burning in the auditorium with subdued lighting and soft music playing.

• If you are talking about an Old Testament celebration or making worship a festive activity, have popcorn popping as people enter, and hand them bags of popcorn to nibble on as they leave the service.

• Have cookies baking as people enter and you talk about having dessert in the desert, making the most of difficult situations.

Taste: "Taste and see that the Lord is good" (Psalm 34:8a).

• The next time you take Communion, emphasize savoring the elements versus gulping them.

• Distribute saltine crackers, and after people eat them, talk about "thirsting" for righteousness.

• A mint can illustrate making our words refreshing.

• Provide tastes of bitter and sweet to illustrate life challenges or change.

• Offer morsels of lamb or elements from the Passover meal when discussing that event.

• Pass a bowl of grapes down the rows when preaching on the Promised Land or John 15.

• Provide cut fruit and toothpicks on platters when the message is about bearing fruit (Galatians 5:22-23).

RELIEVING TENSION

Savvy communicators learn to pick up nonverbal cues when audiences begin to get antsy or wear down, and they move toward tension relief. A sophisticated, motivated audience can handle extended periods of high tension. Their capacity for being engaged over long segments allows a communicator to load up on message protein. Average audiences need carbs every so often. They tire more easily and, therefore, need more frequent tension relief. A communicator can intentionally create emotional rest stops along the message highway, so as not to overtax the audience, in a variety of ways. These pauses in tension are also opportunities to pick up passengers who've checked out because their attention spans have been exhausted.

A tension reliever might be a joke; a simple humorous or whimsical story between points; or a change-of-pace item such as a visual aid, graphic, video clip, or even an audience-participation element. This break in energy flow does not necessarily require a strong tie with the theme. You can create a minor tension reliever nonverbally by stepping out from behind the pulpit/speaker stand or striking a more relaxed, conversational style. If you're using an anecdote, Internet story, or joke, you'll want to tie it to the message as best as you can. But the primary purpose of a tension reliever is not to carry content as much as it is to re-engage people who have become weary in listening and thinking so you can move on to another info chunk without losing them. If the car is pulling the trailer up a long climb, you may have to pull off for a moment to let it rest. A tension reliever may take less than a minute, but it is an important exhale before you subliminally say, "OK, gang, let's get back on the bus. Our trek's not over."

There are obvious benefits of tension relief, but there are also some potential drawbacks. If you spend too much time in relief, it can be more difficult to get everyone on board again. You don't want to veer too far from where you were. We've all heard speakers begin to tell a story or joke and then get carried away. Eventually the listeners ended up thinking, "How did we get here? What does this have to do with the topic?" The speaker wanted to lighten things up a bit or play on a funny story, only to be unable to bring things back to where they were. The risk of overload is very real if you do not relieve tension when it is needed, but you're also vulnerable to losing valuable ground if you deviate too far from the task at hand. That is why message preparation is so important— those who wing it are at great risk here.

THE SILENT KILLER

One of my favorite pastimes is watching movies. My therapist says it's an escape, but what does he know? I call it "sermonic research," although I haven't started taking it off my taxes as a business expense for fear of being audited. Funny word, *movie*. It's a term we still use for the original nickname given to "a moving picture" or "motion picture." Still photos were the best form of visual recording we could hope for until this invention. Moving pictures reflect life more effectively. Consider this when you speak. Why would you want to revert to stationary, static visuals? Granted, your animation as a speaker is far less dramatic than a movie, but the passive, talking-head approach that many pastors take reduces their message reception.

Move around; use arm and hand motions; think about your facial gestures; kneel down; bend over; face people on the left, on the right, and in the center. Communicators who are tied to podiums have to depend solely on the content of their messages, their voices, and their credibility. If you are able, incorporate your face and body to increase energy. You don't have to mimic the old-time, sawdust trail, tent evangelists. Overly animated, melodramatic communicators foaming at the mouth are not what we're recommending. Too many gestures can be distracting.

Vary your volume and pitch. Look natural, not mean or bored. Loosen up. Fake it if you can't feel it. Genuine, natural movement is always preferred over statuelike oratory. Audiences tend to reflect what they see. Speakers often blame their listeners for looking bored, when it's the communicator's responsibility to engage them. We do this subliminally by *how* we present, not just *what* we present.

Think of message presentation as theater. Watch yourself on video to see if you pace unnecessarily or have any irritating gestures or unnecessary animations. If you're talking about joy, smile. If you're discussing something serious, look grim. Practice in the mirror. Before visual electronics, communicators were instructed to exaggerate nonverbal gestures

Group Publishing offers an Advanced Presenters Course to all those who speak in the church. The class includes videotaping student presentations, followed by positive feedback and tips from peers and trained professionals. For more information and a schedule of upcoming courses, see www.grouppublishing.com/summit_experiences.

when speaking to larger crowds. Now, screen projections can amplify our nonverbal communication, much like audio systems do our voices. You may want to consult with a theater teacher or drama coach to give you ideas for improving your nonverbal communication. Message design is not just about construction of content; it's also about presentation efficacy. When we speak with little voice inflection or body animation, we silently kill the energy—thus reducing our connectivity with the audience.

In spite of the influence of television, movies, Internet, and written media, it is amazing how much power public speaking still has. Thomas Long credits Walter Onn, professor of humanities at Saint Louis University and author of *The Presence of the Word*, as saying that "there is nothing more powerful than one person standing up before other people and saying what he or she believes is true. It's more powerful than print, more powerful than television. Nowhere is the person more present than in the spoken word. And people recognize that, and respond."[2] Because of this, we cannot relax our focus on maximizing our presentation skills.

BENEFITS OF PROVIDING MESSAGE OUTLINES FOR NOTE-TAKING

A simple engagement tool that many pastors and teachers use is an outline, with space to encourage receivers to take notes, that people receive prior to a service. While it can be overused, this is generally a good idea because it adds a dimension of audience participation during the message presentation. There are at least ten benefits of using message outlines for note-taking:

1. Provides multi-taskers with something helpful to do as you speak, instead of writing shopping lists or cleaning out their purses.

2. Gives the presenter an opportunity to look at her outline and scan the next few points as people write, cutting down perceived lack of eye contact. This helps cause people to think, "Wow, she rarely looks at her notes."

3. Enhances chances of deeply learning key concepts by adding visual and tactile elements to a primarily audio medium.

4. Provides something to take home for later discussion and pondering, as well as a tool for passing information to others.

5. Taps the curiosity effect as people anticipate the key concepts and empty blanks.

6. The Gutenberg Effect: If it's in print, the information must be more reliable than if it's not.

7. Provides discipline for the presenter to think through concepts and stay on course.

8. Demonstrates organization and added value to receivers—"the speaker has thought this through."

9. Media opportunity to use creative graphics that add complexity and visual appeal to keep people engaged in the message.

10. You can sell really cool, screen-printed, three-ring binders and add a buck or two to the church coffers *(sorry, weak ending point)*.

The perceived benefits of notes are greater if the purpose of the message is to inform, less important if it is to inspire or to persuade (unless the persuasive message relies heavily on apologetics).

Hints for using message outlines well:

• Don't overdo filling in blanks. Instead, ask open-ended questions that encourage the listeners to put the answers in their own words. This forces them to process the questions more deeply.

• Ask questions that are key to understanding the concept and are less likely to be guessed or perceived as irrelevant.

• Don't use outlines just to use them. Some settings don't warrant fill-in-the-blank outlines and may be perceived as gimmicky and frivolous by more sophisticated audiences.

• It's generally better to put the main points into positive, what-to-do terms than to state problems or what not to do.

• Give verbal cues for the answers (for example, "Why was the woman at the well thirsty for spiritual direction?") so people know when to look at their notes and can keep pace. People are distracted when they have to constantly look at their notes for fear of missing or needing to ask someone for the answer they missed.

• Provide sufficient space for normal handwriting, both height and length.

• Double-check with the media portion of the presentation to make sure that what goes on the screen matches the outline. Minor mess-ups detract from the message and cause people to disconnect.

ZAPPING ENERGY DRAINERS

Distractions drain energy from a message by upstaging the speaker. A communicator works hard to connect, but part of that effort needs to go into helping create an environment that has limited distractions. Guest speakers often have to work with what they're given, but most pastors can significantly influence their teaching setting. Here are some common service factors that steal attention from the message goal. While some of these might relate to context and environment factors discussed in Chapter 3, they specifically affect energy level.

Mediocrity: Typos in the handout or projected slides, musical notes gone AWOL, and ho-hum service elements rob quality from the message as well—guilt by association. In *The Five Star Church*, we talk about the importance of doing ministry with excellence—not just for God's glory but also to attract people who are accustomed to quality in other realms of their lives. Mediocrity calls attention to itself and distracts from your message goals.

Service flow: Most pastors are obviously biased toward the spoken word, but what goes on before and after the sermon is also critical to how well people receive the message. Merely plugging a message into a worship service format is blindness. Song selection, prayer, announcements, and other service elements should be designed to prepare hearts and minds to hear well. When they are not, people are distracted before they have a chance to hear you.

Smooth transitions: Churches often drain energy from their people because of poor transitions. Cold stops between songs, boring announcements, and awkward dead time between service elements kill spirit.

Shoot for not more than five seconds of empty time between service elements.

Fill these with musical interludes, graphic or lighting changes, or appropriate narration. Consider instrumental background music during prayer, Scripture, and announcements for ambience. Transition quality can be as important as the elements it connects.

Transition to message: The most important single transition is the one that sets up the message. In the typical Sunday morning worship experience, there's a natural tension relief after the musical segment. This audience exhale is usually healthy prior to the heightened tension created by a well-crafted message opener. But make sure the transition is neutral, not negative. Doing things like announcements or prolonged offering pleas loses what was created during the musical worship and starts the speaker in an energy hole.

Physical matters (people flow, lighting, noise, and so on): We've discussed some of these in terms of setting and creature comforts. Distraction demons are legion when it comes to crowd-control issues. Restroom trips, ringing cell phones, crying or fidgeting kids, and squeaky door hinges can keep people from pondering (or even hearing) the message. Turning heads and wandering eyes pick up motion like a Geiger counter finds radioactivity. Providing non-shadow-casting light on the face of the speaker and the speaker staying within lit boundaries are important. PA systems that work well and people who skillfully adjust them can significantly reduce audio distractions. Dead microphones are irritating and usually preventable. Avoid abrupt sound stops from media by feathering one segment into another like freeway on-ramps.

People moving at inopportune times: Every church is different. Some facilities lend themselves better to reducing distractions than others. The worst times for people to interrupt a message are at the beginning and the end. Do whatever you can to reduce the number of worship-arts or hospitality people moving around during the first and last five minutes. Do not underestimate the energy that is drained by moving people, such as musicians, ushers, attendance counters, and new

All too often, a preacher is someone who talks in other people's sleep.

parents. While it's impossible to impose a lockdown, frequent offenders should be lovingly educated about service protocol for the sake of those around them.

Harry Beckwith wrote, "In communicating, your greatest enemy isn't just the noise all around you—it's the noise you create, unwittingly."[3] William Zinsser wrote, "Noise is the typographical error and the poorly designed page....Ambiguity is noise....Redundancy is noise. Misuse of words is noise. Vagueness is noise. Jargon is noise...Information is your sacred product, and noise is its pollutant. Guard the message with your life."[4]

The role of the church bulletin/worship folder: Once we asked George Barna to visit our services and give us his ideas on what we might do to enhance the effectiveness of our Sunday morning worship experience. George noted that many of our people were not engaged in active worship because they appeared to be distracted by reading their worship folder, filled with church news and upcoming event details. We decided to begin distributing our newsletter handout after the service. Some ministry leaders balked at this idea, suggesting that people would probably not read it after they left church—which only reaffirmed the

"Did you preach on wives being submissive to their husbands again?"

reason to remove this distraction from the worship experience. Instead of handing out a newsletterlike bulletin as people entered, we resorted to a simple handout that included the message outline, some application ideas, and a few pre-service helps for meditating and Scripture reading.

Since then we've modified that slightly to include a brief list of "main events" that pertain to items or events that people may need to know before leaving campus for the day. All other materials and advertisements are handed out as people leave. We've replaced nearly all hand-outs and mail-outs with a weekly electronic broadcast newsletter that is also available on our Web site, saving money and labor. We keep all information in hard-copy form for the few who like it this way. But we've learned not to diminish the hard work we put into connecting with people through our message by providing them with distractions.

Every service and message has energy rhythms to it— ebbing and flowing levels of engagement. Effective communicators manage this energy flow in their messages so they don't lose listeners with too little or too much tension.

Discussion/Thought Prompters

1. Take your most current message, and plot a visual graph that you think depicts its energy.
2. What did you use to relieve tension? Did it seem to work well for that purpose?
3. Take the same message, and determine whether or not you began with your second best point and ended with your strongest point. What would you change?
4. What are common, known distractions within your ministry setting? What can you do to reduce them?
5. What was the most helpful idea in this chapter?

Chapter Eight

Secret #8

Ask for the Sale

KEEP THE GOAL IN SIGHT

"He's at the forty, the thirty, the twenty, the ten. He's headed for the end zone...Ohhh, tackled on the one yard line."

That's how a lot of messages end up; the communicator runs it down the field but fails to cross the goal line.

Haddon Robinson wrote, "Like a lawyer, a minister asks for a verdict. The congregation should see the idea entire and complete, and listeners should know and feel what God's truth demands of them. Directly or indirectly the conclusion answers the question, So what?"[1]

Just as a trial lawyer pleads a case for a verdict, a pastor should preach for response. Effective communicators cultivate environments in which responses are normal and expected—because good communicators tend to develop good audiences. I can usually tell when people are used to having a good communicator because they are good listeners. There's a spirit of anticipation. People tend to laugh more, smile, nod their heads, and provide nonverbal feedback indicating that they're ready to listen and learn.

Conversely, audiences that are hungry for good communication are still often lethargic and apathetic because they're not anticipating much. By improving your communication, you enhance the ongoing responsiveness of your receivers. This in turn affords you greater opportunities to create response options, increasing the chances of listeners applying your message.

George Sweazey, former preaching professor at Princeton Theological Seminary wrote, "The conclusion is burdened with two handicaps: The minister prepares it when he is the most tired, and the congregation hears it when they are the most tired."[2]

Pilots tell you that the trickiest part of any flight is the landing. Make sure you put plenty of energy into finishing well, both as you create your message and when you present it to the receivers. Consider making the conclusion one of the first parts you write, as you think through what you want the message to accomplish.

EVERY COMMUNICATOR IS IN SALES

If you need a pen, look for a salesman. The good ones always have a pen close at hand. They're ready to ink a deal. Effective communicators are willing to ask for commitment. When you design a message, you need to consider where you want to go and what you're looking for from the receivers. You are not just the manufacturer and distributor. You're also into sales. That may be the last thing most pastors think about themselves, but it's true.

To *sell* means "convincing that results in response." When Paul spoke to King Agrippa, he didn't close the deal, but apparently he asked for it because the king responded, "Do you think you can make me a Christian so quickly?" (Acts 26:28, NLT). Junk mail is considered garbage because it arrives without affecting us. Effective communication always influences us in some way.

Some of the most hypocritical communicators are in mass media. Out of one side of their mouths, they claim no responsibility for the social behavior of people who emulate what they see on their programs. "We don't make people kill each other. We don't tell them to have affairs. We don't cause teens to do drugs." But then they turn around and tell

> "It's said that Adlai Stevenson, when complimented on a speech, once pointed out that people often said what nice speeches he made, but that after John F. Kennedy's speeches they said, 'Let's march!' "
>
> —Suzette Elgin[3]

vendors, "Buy ads because we can significantly increase your sales." They avoid responsibility when it is inconvenient but sell the power of persuasion when it is in their favor. Effective communication influences us. Effective communicators understand this and work to harvest the results.

THERE ARE THREE THINGS YOU SELL AS A PREACHER

You're selling yourself. Read Zig Ziglar or any sales guru, and he'll tell you that everyone is in sales. If nothing else, we're selling ourselves. While this sounds a bit narcissistic, the essence of the principle is that people aren't willing to listen to those they don't take seriously. When you dated your mate, you were selling yourself and your potential. Jesus could not do miracles in his hometown because the people there didn't buy into his messianic ministry. To a certain degree, you cannot separate the message from the messenger. How we are perceived colors what we say. Communicators who pretend not to care what people think about them undermine their message. We're not talking about egotism but legitimate awareness of source credibility and dependability.

You're selling your message. Most of us can more easily see how communicators are salespeople in terms of purveying ideas. When we were looking for a stewardship company to help us raise capital funds for our church, we narrowed our list to two groups. A representative of each came to our leaders to pitch his company's service. While I think that the organizations are probably equally reputable, one won hands down because of the rep's ability to communicate well.

The power of the principles you teach is life-changing. You believe that, but many in your audience are less convinced. You are selling the ideas, their practicality in everyday life, and why people should prioritize them highly.

You're selling God. As a minister, you're selling more than yourself and your message. As a representative of God, you are re-presenting him to people who've either forgotten him, never known him,

> *"If you cry 'Forward!' you must without fail make it plain in what direction to go. Don't you see that if, without doing so, you call out the word to both a monk and a revolutionary, they will go in directions precisely opposite?"*
> —ANTON CHEKHOV[4]

or are learning more about him. The passion and quality with which you communicate your message, in addition to the content itself, leave an impression that will either endear people to Christ and his claims or leave them no better off. Right or wrong, people tend to develop opinions of God based on your believability as his vendors.

TELL THEM WHAT YOU'RE LOOKING FOR

How will they know unless we tell them? Most of the time, people need ideas about what they should do with the message you're providing. It's not that they're stupid or unmotivated, but when they leave the message, their context changes. The seed you've planted is apt to be bombarded with weeds, competing with the young sprouts for nutrients. The best place to give people ideas on how they can apply today's truth is in the message itself. The principle of stewardship means that we're responsible for the outcome of our talent. We can't bury it, assuming it's safe and that we've done our job. Why would we go to all the work of designing and presenting a message only to drop the ball when it comes to asking for the sale? There are four main reasons:

Fear of failure or rejection: The biggest single hindrance to professional sales people is the fear of rejection. Separating our self-esteem from the decisions of others is difficult. We give it our best shot and then, after all our work and effort, fail to convince. Paul couldn't fully persuade Agrippa. Jesus didn't convince everyone who heard him. That didn't prevent him from saying, "Take up your cross and follow me" (Luke 9:23). By avoiding drawing the line in the sand, we deceive ourselves into thinking we've succeeded because we have nothing to tell us otherwise. Obviously, this is not true. Good communicators take the risk of asking for a response.

Lack of clarity: Sometimes we don't ask for a response because what we're looking for is cloudy in our own minds. We have a hard time establishing a real-life application because we've not pondered the pragmatic outcome of our message. When the communicator isn't clear on the practical ramifications of his or her message, it will be very difficult to convey realistic response ideas toreceivers.

Fear of success/challenge of follow-through: It sounds funny to fear success, but with it comes new responsibilities. Sometimes we don't ask for the sale because the extra effort adds difficulty to our work. It's often easier to give people the message and let them determine their own response to it. If people are interested in becoming Christians or rededicating or forming a small group, it may mean follow-up calls, counseling, developing materials, training, and so on. By avoiding the *ask*, we lessen our workload. It's equivalent to a salesperson avoiding paperwork by scuttling a deal.

Finding appropriate response ideas: Sometimes we don't ask for the sale because it seems we can't determine an adequate response. Coming up with creative approaches for people to say "yes" to God is often challenging, if we take it seriously. The two options are to either do nothing or have people come forward to pray or be prayed for by someone else. Generic invitations fit a decreasing number of people these days and do not necessarily do justice to your message theme. Other options are the raising of hands, going to a designated prayer area after the service, picking up and taking home an item provided at the exit, or marking a communication card.

PREACH TOWARD RESPONSE

What are you preaching or teaching toward? When you arrive, how will you know when you've gotten there? What kind of attitudes, behaviors, or next steps will reflect the kind of progress you're seeking? Or are you just shooting the breeze because that's what you're paid to do?

"Ask and it will be given to you; seek and you will find; knock and the door will be opened to you" (Matthew 7:7). That's not just an admonition for pursuing God. It's also a truth about life in general. The people who articulate what they're looking for and go after it are consistently more productive than those who do not. If you don't preach toward response, then why do you preach at all?

The goal of most messages is to improve receivers' lives, deepen their faith, or enhance their relationships. Conveying Bible content as an end unto itself is not good stewardship. Our goal must be life transformation. For most of us, transformation begins with baby steps. The progressive pilgrimage toward godliness is filled with ideas and experiences that mark our lives for the better. A benefit of communicating for a response is that we gain a sense of progress along that path. Spiritual formation and personal maturity are tedious, messy processes. We don't see a quarterly profit-and-loss statement as in business or tangible products as in construction and manufacturing.

All of us are motivated by results. Inner travel should result in outer steps. By creating response opportunities, we can get a feel for the receptivity of our people as well as their spiritual progress. Obviously you can't measure all growth outwardly. You can also distort feedback by establishing inappropriate responses or manipulating them. But healthy, consistent response opportunities as part of your messages serve as vehicles for ingraining principles in people's lives.

ORGANIC DECISIONS

"Home of the No-Haggle Car Deal," says the auto dealership sign. People are tired of high-pressured sales, manipulation, and stressful shopping experiences. More car lots are moving toward the noncommissioned, sticker-price approach. Online shopping is growing every year, in part because people don't have to hassle with salespeople who seem either unhelpful or pushy. Today's receivers have little tolerance for singing twenty stanzas of "Just as I Am." Having started out in ministry as an evangelist who spoke in settings in which altar calls were expected, the unspoken idea was that if no one came forward, you must not have done your job. While you were never officially on commission, the more who came forward, the better. Veterans of the trade could milk an altar call for all its worth, often crossing the line of authentic movement of the Spirit by wearing down the emotions governing free will.

Today's local church is more like an orchard. People come and soak in the atmosphere of God and his truth as they progressively move toward a decision. As a result, their decisions are more apt to last over the long haul. Fruit picked too green often fails to ripen and ends up rotting. Spiritual decisions are induced prematurely usually don't mature into rich fruit that reproduces. Those who study the science of persuasion realize that people tend to move one

Never preach to preach. Give 'em heaven!

notch at a time toward a belief. Otherwise they develop buyer's remorse and end up returning their purchase. While pastors should preach toward response, try to do more than a traditional altar call or public invitation to come forward. Contemporary pastors are sometimes confronted by traditionalists who assume that the only place to receive Christ is after the message during a formal invitation. "How do people accept Christ if you don't offer an altar call?" they sincerely ask. The best response may be in the form of another question: "How have people throughout history made decisions to follow Christ?"

The contemporary version of the altar call is a relatively modern invention in church life. John Wesley is credited with creating the prayer bench (1700s), which evolved into the place to "do business with God." Evangelists such as Billy Sunday, D.L. Moody, and Billy Graham popularized the practice, to the point that evangelical Christians in the twentieth century have come to assume it is the primary way to invite Christ into one's life.

But name a single biblical reference that emulates the modern version of a church invitation, where people walk to the front to pray and receive Christ. How have people crossed the line of commitment throughout history? They've done it in homes and restaurants, alone on retreats, in casual conversations with friends, after prayer or Bible studies, during worship services, and any number of situations, both formal and informal.

Organic decision-making means you let fruit ripen on the vine instead of picking it green. While today's receivers are a bit more skeptical and tend to smell the scent of manipulation a mile away, this does not mean we never try for a harvest. Organic fruit still gets picked, when it is ready. The overcompensation for high-pressure spiritual selling is no pressure at all. The trick, if there is one, is to provide a low-grade pressure that does not feel like pressure because it's done without manipulation. It comes in the form of an idea, suggestion, or education. Teachers and educators are most definitely influencers, but they sell their ideas without being perceived as salesmen. This is at times the subtlest form of selling: when you don't realize you're being sold.

Sometimes when I speak, I blow it. I get to the end and wind up missing a perfect opportunity to invite people to take a step forward spiritually. Maybe I fail to listen to the Spirit as closely as I should, feel rushed by time, neglect planning for a response, or just get sidetracked and forget. I cringe when I realize I didn't ask for the sale as I might have.

> *All communication is a form of persuasion: "Listen to me."*

A recent example occurred after a message on Philemon, which focused on the power of accountability and community. Because of intimate Christian community, Paul could confront Onesimus to do the right thing in returning to his owner, Philemon. He named Philemon's family and friends and asked him to do the right thing when his runaway slave returned. At the same time, we were promoting our small-group ministry. I intended to ask people to circle C on their communication cards so that we could follow up, but I forgot. After the service, one of our leaders said it would have been a great time to ask people for commitment. "You left money on the table," he said, and I agreed. I missed a great opportunity to engage a response that would allow us to follow up with people and recommend a specific small group.

RESPONSE IDEAS

A potential downside of providing specific response ideas is reductionism—giving the impression that a concept can be summed up with an exact behavior or that we've fixed a deep problem with a magic wand of raising a hand, filling out a response card, or coming forward to pray. As long as you're aware of the danger (and you might even mention this as a disclaimer from time to time), you need not fear this risk. The other side of this concern is being so broad that every message ends up with a generic conclusion: "Accept Christ," "Get closer to God," "Be more committed." Traditional conservatism suggests that you should never let a message go by without giving people an opportunity to accept Christ, so that whether you're talking about Christian community, holiness, or stewardship, you turn it into an evangelistic opportunity. While this sounds good (Who could say no to inviting folks into the kingdom?), a response that is not true to the message will be seen as inauthentic and potentially manipulative. The goal is life transformation more than decisions. You can have the latter without dramatic instances of the former.

The good news is that people today want to respond. We live in an experiential society, in which people discover their "truth" by living it. That's how they come to know their "truth." Call for commitment with boldness and confidence but not guilt or pushiness. People can smell fear. If you come across as insecure or hesitant, people will mirror what they see. Graciously give people an opportunity to put feet to their faith and demonstrate their spiritual growth.

Cultural analysts agree that we're in an experiential society in which people want to do more than just spectate; they want to participate and respond. At the same time, people are averse to feeling manipulated or forced to respond in a certain way. The key is variety and appropriateness. Here are ways to ask for a response:

- **Mark communication cards/tearaway bulletin slips.**

Having a response card or slip of paper is a great tool for people to communicate questions, prayer requests, and responses. It gives them something to "do" to register their inward growth. I recommend including this in the offering so people can conveniently submit the cards. That is why we prefer to take offerings at the end of the service, so people can register decisions made after the message. (This also allows guests more time to fill out registration and interest information.) The offering becomes a means of worship with money and recorded responses.

- **Creative action options:**

—One week action meant going to a Communion station placed on the perimeter of the auditorium.

—One time we had a banner with the photo of our new building on it, on which people wrote the names of their lost friends and associates they hoped would come to know Christ in our new worship center, thus emphasizing people over bricks and mortar.

—After a Good Friday service, people wrote on index cards things they had been forgiven of and then walked outside to nail them on a large cross in the courtyard. The sound of pounding nails was powerful in that solemn moment.

—Once everyone received a small stone when they entered the auditorium. The message was about forgiveness. At the end of the service, we invited people to come forward and put their stones on the front of the platform (instead of throwing them at someone).

—After a message about God meeting our needs, we invited people to come forward to drink from one of three water coolers that had been marked as *love, faith,* or *wisdom.* People filled small cups of water from the coolers that represented their needs and drank the water.

• **Sign-ups:** If the talk is on helping the needy, provide a table in the lobby for people to sign up to feed the homeless. If small group community is the theme, have information on your groups available. Take advantage of people's immediate interest by putting something in their hands and giving them an opportunity to sign up after the presentation.

• **Go to a certain area after the service.** Sometimes a message will move people to sense a need for prayer, counsel, or sharing. Our church has a prayer area that is marked in one corner of the auditorium. Convenient go-to places that are staffed with sensitive people who'll encourage responders is a beneficial option.

"Let your yea be yea, your nay be nay, and your 'in conclusion' be your conclusion."

Dennis Fletcher, 17 Ruth Dr., Monroe City, MO 63456, dfletch76@socket.net. Used by artist's permission. Reprinted from Leadership Journal.

• **Stand/raise hand:** Although this is a standard, it can be fresh if presented as a response option—an outward demonstration of an inward decision. The key is to try to avoid a situation in which people feel guilty if they don't stand (for example, "Stand if you want to take God seriously in your life"). Provide ample disclaimers for those who aren't ready. Acknowledge that if you felt today's message was specifically for you for whatever reason, you may want to respond. This winnows out those who feel bad if they don't respond to everything, every time. After seeking a visual response, invite people to note that via the communication card.

• **Assignments:** We discussed take-home application ideas earlier. Print practical ways of implementing a key concept during the coming week. It may be an anonymous act of kindness, calling a relative, writing the name of a lost person on a prayer list, or writing an answer to a question.

Although you can't be sure who'll apply the truth outside of the service, you can enhance the rate and depth of commitment by offering opportunities to respond to a message. Preaching for response implies you have done your work in message creation and believe the Holy Spirit will work in hearts as you speak. It also reinforces in the minds of your receivers that you're interesting in growing their souls, and so are they.

Discussion/Thought Prompters

1. What is your ministry culture's tradition regarding message responses?
2. What are the pros and cons of this style?
3. What kind of response can you ask for during your next message? How will this help those who respond? Does this require follow-up from you or staff?
4. What do you think is the biggest challenge in "asking for the sale"?
5. What from this chapter helped you most?

Chapter Nine
Secret #9

Measure Results

GOOD ENOUGH NEVER IS

One might think that with so much effort going into designing a message, a communicator would be finished once the product is delivered. But effective communicators understand that "good enough" never is. The goal is not perfection because, in an art form like communication, subjectivity prevents us from ever accomplishing perfection. Excellence, on the other hand, must be our goal as stewards of God's call. Every week pastors must at some point make the decision to pull the plug on further message creation (even if it's during the last song before the message). A message isn't like the vintage cars in garages across America that sit around for years of spare-time tinkering. We have to drive our message out on the road every week, ready or not. To continue to improve, we need to gather feedback to show us where we can invest our energy for maximum impact.

Without an active feedback system, we can't be confident that our design efforts are being effective and that our messages are connecting with receivers. So if feedback is so important, why do few of us actively seek it? There are three main reasons:

1. We're too pooped from creation and delivery to delve deeply into assessment. Besides, with all that's going on, next week is here before we know it, and who has the time to linger on leftovers?

2. We're unfamiliar with feedback and assessment tools that might

help us. We rely on our own sense of effectiveness and an occasional comment at the door as parishioners head for the parking lot. Then there is the infamous Monday commentary from our spouses (which they've likely tempered over the years in order to ensure marital harmony).

3. We're unwilling to look at ourselves in the mirror, lest we dislike what we see. It's easer to hope for the best and assume we're doing OK than face our own ineffectiveness. Even humble servants of Christ have egos, causing us to avoid possible weak points in a particular message or, worse, continue to make message-creation errors.

Certainly we can see how we'd benefit from periodic assessment, but what's the difference between feedback for improvement and giving people a license to change the way we preach? Isn't there a danger that we'll end up only giving them what they want—you know, ear-tickling messages?

> You're going to find that there will be times when people will have no stomach for solid teaching, but will fill up on spiritual junk food— catchy opinions that tickle their fancy. They'll turn their backs on truth and chase mirages. But you—keep your eye on what you're doing; accept the hard times along with the good; keep the Message alive; do a thorough job as God's servant (2 Timothy 4:3-5, *The Message*).

Don't give them what they want. Give them what they *need* in a *way* they want. The bottom line is that you will have to discern what God wants you to say and how to say it. Gathering feedback helps reveal what you may be missing. Communicators sometimes think a certain gesture, joke, or style of presentation is more effective than it really is. We may be oblivious to a mannerism, habit, or gesture that is an irritation to our listeners. Out of respect, people may never mention it, feeling it is not their place or assuming they might hurt your feelings. Relationships in the local church often take precedence over honesty. This can be good, and it can be bad. It is dysfunctional to put up with someone's shortcomings to the detriment of others and even the person. Tough love requires us to confront unhealthy actions and attitudes. Performance and productivity are important to staff and ministry teams. If we never confront or critique a team member because we're concerned about being a "good family member," we fail that person.

Obviously, the key is balance. By avoiding truth-telling and constructive feedback, we hinder our stewardship. If we constantly nitpick and criticize, we kill people's spirits. They're rendered useless if they withhold their gifts or quit. Communicators who desire to connect develop assertive yet healthy feedback systems. Improving our craft is a lifelong process. While many with talent and experience get by without ever seeking input from others, they end up being less than they could have been because they don't continue to develop that talent. Let's look at some ideas for developing healthy feedback and measurement instruments to help you grow in your effectiveness as a communicator.

FEEDBACK TOOLS

The reason you can't rely on church-door feedback is that it tends to be "church nice" and nonspecific. Some days I laugh. After an especially strong service, I'll receive five times as many comments on my shirt, hair, or weight loss than on message content. In spite of hours of preparation effort, people focus on silly, trivial matters. It's polite, social, small talk. They may mention a joke or illustration but rarely talk about how their hearts moved or they made a deep spiritual decision. This doesn't mean they're not responding, only that post-service lobby interaction does not lend itself to that sort of feedback. Rushed listening prevents deep sharing. Then there is the political correctness that endangers adequate feedback. People don't want to offend you or say something that may strain their relationship with you. Add to that the inaccurate feedback due to limited reflection, and you are lucky to get anything redeemable for improving your communication.

Then there's the church critic, whose self-professed calling is to speak his or her mind, regardless of the pain it may cause. These well-intentioned dragons confuse healthy feedback with negativity and condition us to avoid message feedback. "You shouldn't have said this..." "Why did you say it like that?" "I don't like it when..." "You should..." By proactively establishing healthy feedback systems, we can often head off the reactive types and take the wind out of their sails.

Personal review: You'll likely grimace when you read this, but one of the simplest methods for improvement is to listen to your own message recordings, as well as watch yourself on videotape. Would you rather scratch your fingernails on a chalkboard than pop in a video or audio recording of last week's sermon? Join the club. But seeing and hearing ourselves gives us better perspective than merely answering the question "How did you feel things went today?" Try to do this on a quarterly basis. If you're concentrating on improving specific things, weekly assessment may be helpful. Athletic coaches use game reviews as part of their improvement strategies. Using recordings along with other feedback can maximize your impact.

Feedback team: Ask individuals in your congregation to serve on a feedback team. Ask two to six people to provide specific feedback on your messages. You can let them determine their own note-taking format, provide an outline of your message to follow and make comments in the margins, or provide a feedback form similar to the one on page 125. (The questions on page 125 are merely suggestions. You can develop your own feedback report, based on what you're striving to measure. See Appendix A (p. 172) for a Message Connectivity Assessment (MCA) based on the principles discussed in this book.)

Pastor Wayne Klemper didn't respond well to criticism.

Used by artist's permission. Reprinted from Leadership Journal.

MESSAGE FEEDBACK

Can you do me a big favor? In order to help our church continually improve the impact of its ministry, I'd personally appreciate your loving but honest feedback on today's message. Please respond to this survey, put it in the attached envelope, and return it to the church office. Thanks in advance for your willingness to do this.

—Pastor

DATE:_____

MESSAGE TITLE/THEME:_____

(For questions asking you to circle a number, use 1 as low and 5 as high)

1. Rate how the service transitioned from the first parts to the message. (Any ideas on how to improve this?) 1 2 3 4 5

2. Rate the introduction. Did it gain your attention and explain the purpose of the message? 1 2 3 4 5

3. Rate the structure in terms of clear main points. 1 2 3 4 5

4. Rate the message's transitions. (Did they seem to flow well from point to point? Was there a specific transition that seemed confusing or rough?) 1 2 3 4 5

5. Which point or illustration got your attention or made a lot of sense?

6. What point or illustration was confusing or didn't seem to fit?

7. What is one thing you specifically gained from today's message?

8. Rate the pastor's perceived passion for today's message and give reasons for this rating. 1 2 3 4 5

9. Rate the relevance of the message to your life. 1 2 3 4 5

10. Rate the relevance of today's message to the other listeners. (How might this be improved?) 1 2 3 4 5

11. Were there any distractions that drew your attention away from the message?

12. Rate the closing and give ideas for improvement. 1 2 3 4 5

Observer's name: (Optional, but helpful if we need clarification.)

> Defensiveness *is*
> *another word for*
> deafness.

By hand-selecting individuals to do this on a periodic basis, you develop rapport and train them to provide helpful feedback (not "I enjoyed it very much"). The downside of using the same people is that you run the risk of developing professional critics who are unable to listen to a message without critiquing it and who see you as a subject for their correction. Periodic, random invitations before a service for a few people to fill out feedback reports can be effective, and it avoids this elite critique attitude. Review comments a couple of days after Sunday, when you're in a good frame of mind.

Church shopper: Ask someone to come in and assess your communication incognito. This could be a person in the community who matches your church's target group, a friend, or a professional speech coach whose assignment is to provide both positive and negative—but constructive—critique. Review that person's notes along with a video/audio recording so you can better understand what he or she is saying. A third party, unfamiliar with you or your church, can often hear and see from unique angles and provide ideas for improvement.

There is a tenuous balance between retaining your authority as God's Word-bearer and being the object of subjective advice-giving from others. No one enjoys being judged, but (whether you seek it or not) know that you are, so you may as well benefit from the feedback. Ironically, if we use this to improve our effectiveness, we inevitably reduce the informal criticism that goes on without our knowledge.

Don't just look at comments specific to a single message; be on the lookout for trends. This means you'll need to do this a number of times. You must develop your personal style. There will be messages that connect with certain people because that's where they are in their lives. There will be other days when a message falls flat or only a few people need to hear it. Don't overemphasize any individual criticism, but listen intently to items you hear over and over. These will usually reveal the areas that you need to work on in order to be more effective.

While it's certainly not scientific, my theory is that on any given Sunday, 10 to 20 percent of the people specifically need to hear the message you've prepared. The Holy Spirit will use it to convey truths applicable to their current needs. Approximately 60 percent of receivers will benefit, but not with a sense of urgency. The remaining 10 to 20 percent probably didn't need to hear the message because of where they are in their walk, at least at this time. Keeping this in mind helps temper some of the feedback, both positive and negative, as we weigh its value.

Most people will respect you for seeking their opinions. They are apt to esteem you for striving to improve and will tend to value your preaching all the more. Certainly there are exceptions, and most of us will discern the personalities in our congregations who cannot handle the responsibility of providing constructive feedback. There are also people whose feedback will be unhelpful because they are biased toward (or against) us or are unable to articulate their ideas.

All feedback is not created equal. Listen more intently to those who are in the center of your target market and those who have proven to have your best interests in mind. Friends and family members should be heard well. Just this last evening, after a Bible study, my wife and I got into our car to drive to another church event. She said, "I don't mean to be critical or anything, but you've kind of gotten into the bad habit of saying 'you know' a lot."

"I don't always understand what he's trying to say, but he loves everyone, is good with kids, and you should see him catch a Frisbee!"

Ouch. That smarted. Didn't she know I was in the middle of writing a great book on communicating? I have been preaching for over two decades and have a graduate degree in communication psychology. Who is she to critique me?

She is my longtime, loyal wife who wants me to be at my best. I gulped and said, "Oh, no. I am? I hadn't noticed."

"It's probably just filler," she said.

"OK, thanks. I'll try to be aware of that. I hate to pick up a bad habit. Just let me know when I do," I said, truly grateful for the feedback, even though a bit embarrassed.

Discussion/Thought Prompters

1. What feedback system/tool have you relied on in the past?
2. When is the last time you listened to or watched a recording of your preaching?
3. List people you'd like to recruit for your input team.
4. Who should you avoid putting on such a team?
5. What will you do to measure feedback on your next message?

Chapter Ten

Secret #10

Bridge for Broader
Impact

YET ANOTHER REFORMATION

S ecret #10 is aimed squarely at the unique conditions in America in the early twenty-first century. Less than 5 percent of the 300,000 plus congregations in America are growing because of evangelism. Those who want to do so are going to have to learn to speak two languages at the same time: churched and unchurched. This latter group can be referred to as seekers, spiritual explorers, pre-Christians, unchurched, or irreligious. A subgroup might be called the dechurched—those who were raised in the church but who disconnected after leaving home, primarily due to perceived irrelevance.

There is a myth that you cannot communicate with those who are spiritual explorers at the same time you're speaking to established Christians. The idea is that you need distinct worship service experiences for each group. While some churches focus on seekers on the weekend and believers midweek, a growing number of congregations are discovering that this

> *"Our task is to enable God's revealed truth to flow out of the Scriptures into the lives of the men and women of today…It is across this broad and deep divide of two thousand years of changing culture (more still in the case of the Old Testament) that Christian communicators have to throw bridges."*
> —JOHN STOTT[1]

> *The big question is "Do you want to be a pastor or a missionary?" The need is far greater for missionaries—those willing to speak the indigenous language to reach people.*

bifocal approach to ministry is not necessary, as long as the communicator is able to walk the fine line between these two groups.

I interrupted work on this chapter to see the movie *Luther*. This moving epic on the life of Martin Luther inspired me with a timeless truth: Communicating in the common language of the day is integral to people understanding the gospel. As Luther labored to translate the New Testament into German so ordinary people could read Scriptures in their native language, he said, "The language of the Bible should be like a mother talking to her children."[2]

Today over half a billion people attend churches that resulted from the Reformation. A part of ongoing reform involves keeping Scriptures understandable. Eugene Peterson did this well as he wrote *The Message* in everyday English. A friend of mine, Terry Crist, wrote a book titled *Learning the Language of Babylon*, referring to our need to both understand and speak to the culture in which we minister. The job of pastors today is to use terms that the pre-Christians understand, while also addressing the already convinced.

WHAT SEEKERS WANT AND NEED

Seekers want to understand God in terms they comprehend. Most fall into three categories: those who have no church background, those who have had negative church experience(s), or those who have a positive church heritage from which they've strayed. Phillip Yancey said that in the latter two cases, it's more like "dating a virgin versus a divorce." The latter groups have heard the love-God talk before.[3] As we've said, most of them have not rejected God as much as their inaccurate perceptions of God, Jesus, and the church. People who are tire-kicking Christianity want to see if this belief system works and how it might improve their lives. They begin with their felt needs. They are open to heavy, honest truth, as long as it's not jammed down their throats or presented in a way that seems to negate their free will to participate or not. The contemporary idea that absolute truth does not exist means that if our approach appears autocratic or exclusive, they'll tend to reject the message. Seekers today want God to make sense. They realize their need for spiritual growth, but if it sounds like the church of their past—which they dismissed as irrelevant—we'll fail to connect.

Seekers have the same needs as every person throughout history: a personal relationship with God through Christ. They, like we, have soul holes that yearn to be filled. These inner cavities desire love, peace, fulfillment, meaning, and purpose. Nothing has changed in our spiritual nature that renders the Bible obsolete or the basic truths of Christ irrelevant. Those who've never personalized their commitment to Christ or been effectively discipled come to church with shallow doctrinal knowledge. We must meet them where they are. These people yearn for the truth but are unable to see how a Christian belief system is able to fill their soul holes.

Effective communicators today cannot afford to dive deeply into doctrinal and denominational distinctions in most large-crowd situations. Perhaps these were options in earlier times when most people were saturated in the basics, but even then one might question the benefit of public monologues on doctrinal fine points. These matters are usually best taught in classroom settings where there can be feedback and discussion.

There is much talk in America about what postmodernism is. Even the term suggests that we don't know what it is, as much as we realize it's different from modernity. A friend of mine just returned from studying at Oxford during his sabbatical. He said in Europe, postmodern conversations are almost passé. The description of postmodernity is primarily one of humanism and secularism. So how do we connect with pre-Christians in this environment?

Real's the deal: Only time will tell if reality television programming will be a fad or an enduring entertainment option. What these programs reflect is society's desire for authenticity. Pretense and polish are cast off because they fail to reflect the real world. Everyday life is itself a drama if we approach it the right way. People have little tolerance for sugar-coated, highly polished God-talk. "Give me the real deal," they demand. "Don't talk ivory tower theology." People want to see you and life as they really are, warts and all.

131

In the mid-1980s, some researchers at Cleveland State University made a startling discovery.

The researchers created two fictitious job candidates—Dave and John—two identical résumés, and two almost identical letters of reference. The only difference was that John's letter included the sentence "Sometimes, John can be difficult to get along with."

The researchers showed the résumés to personnel directors. Which candidate did the directors most want to interview?

Sometimes-Difficult-to-Get-Along-With John.

The researchers concluded that the criticism of John made the references' praise of John seem more believable, and that made John look like a strong candidate. Showing John's warts actually helped sell John.[4]

This gives us the opportunity to address controversial subjects because they tend to be the most real. How we deal with them is the key. Black-and-white answers tend to be rejected. Hues of gray are the preferred chromatic scheme of today's messages. That doesn't nullify truth or hope but acknowledges the messiness of life. If you don't understand something, admit it. If there are no clear-cut answers to a problem, say it. If all your stories have a happy ending, you'll be rejected as fake.

Honest yet tender: Jesus' style of communicating is the most effective for today's seeker audience. He never compromised on the truth. His values were conservative, yet his approach to people was quite liberal. You can confront the issue of homosexuality, as long as you're loving toward homosexuals. You can address illicit sex, but you can't do so with a stone in your hand. The key is attitude. Far too often we've confused approval of a belief or behavior with acceptance of a person. The only people Jesus seemed to reject were those who condemned others and failed to exude a grace-filled attitude. Tell it like it is, but do so without finger-pointing. You can even tell people that you're sorry you have to raise an issue, but because it's your job and it's in the Bible, you have to do it in spite of your discomfort. There's a difference between exuding confidence and condemning.

In The Search for Signs of Intelligent Life in the Universe, *Lily Tomlin offers an understandable reaction to the last fifty years:*
" 'I worry that no matter how cynical you become,' she says, 'you still can't keep up.' "[5]

I recently presented a message that took a somewhat confrontational look at passive parenting, in the context of King David's dysfunctional family matters. I listed some of the excuses parents use for not taking their kids to church. I said, "It bugs me when parents say, 'I can't get them out of bed.' It bugs me when I hear them say, 'I don't want to push my beliefs on them.' " I asked my wife how it came across since it was a pretty strong approach. She graciously said, "It was good. I liked it. I just wish you'd have said, 'It *hurts me* when I hear' instead of 'it *bugs me* when I hear.' You don't want people to feel like they can't be honest with you or that you'll reject them if they don't measure up." It was a good suggestion of how to slightly reword a statement to exude grace instead of condemnation.

Provide an exit: Absolute truth is nonexistent in the minds of most unchurched people today. This growing mind-set is alien to those within evangelical circles and, really, all of traditional Western thinking. It seems to allow a person to embrace contradictory ideas without experiencing inner conflict. Pluralism is in vogue—the acceptance of multiple truths rather than only one. This doesn't mean you as a preacher can't speak truth or that you have to water down messages. It only means that you must provide a disclaimer that says in effect, "You don't have to believe this. You can accept or reject it. But this is what the Bible teaches. This is a non-negotiable of the Christian belief system. If you accept or reject Christianity, you should do so from an informed position."

By saying this, are you really saying anything new? You aren't. People have always had the right to choose not to believe in Christianity, but you've just reminded them of this option without compromising God's Word in the process.

People also do not buy into the idea that the Bible is the primary source of truth. "When evangelicals insist that the Bible must be accepted as

> *"One reason the Christian worldview is so highly criticized in a postmodern context lies in the apparent Christian unwillingness to coexist with any other viewpoint. Christians are then perceived to be threatened and incapable of dealing with a person's refusal to embrace our way of thinking."*
> —GRAHAM JOHNSTON[6]

authoritative before the book can even be read, postmoderns feel pressured to make a huge leap of faith—and they won't do it. The focus of the biblical communicator must shift from asking, 'How do I protect the Bible from people viewing it as just another book?' to a more strategic issue, 'How can I get them to examine the Bible to see if it is true?' "[7]

Tolerance is revered, so if you disclaim other belief systems or doctrinal distinctions, you must do so with a gracious attitude. This is what Paul did on Mars Hill within that polytheistic culture. Attitude and style are the keys to doing this so that postmoderns won't tune you out. If your attitude is judgmental and condemning, if your style is autocratic and sectarian, people will not listen. If they smell intolerance in your message, they'll unplug. The beauty of this contemporary value is that it opens the door for you to speak openly and boldly about biblical matters, as long as you present it as an option. Sharing "your truth" is in vogue. Faith is the solution anyway. Giving the impression that Christianity is the only belief system will inevitably backfire, even though by faith we believe it's the only one worth following.

The pursuit of inquiry: Because truth does not exist in the mind of the postmodern, there's no room for dogmatic statements. The teaching approach must move toward the Socratic, whereby questions implore the receiver to engage in the investigation process. One reason corporate coaching has become such a popular skill in recent years is the sense that people have the answers within them as long as the coach asks the right questions. Ancient teachers such as Socrates and Jesus used dialogue to ask questions, and large group communicators can accomplish the same thing today by coaxing interest from listeners with comments such as "Have you ever wondered…?" "Some of you are

"We preach biblically. Why, of course; how else could we preach?…But if I were to draw a diagram of the gulf between the two worlds, and then plot our sermons on the diagram, I would have to draw a straight line which begins in the biblical world, and then goes up in the air on a straight trajectory, but never lands on the other side. For our preaching is seldom if ever earthed. It fails to build a bridge into the modern world. It is biblical, but not contemporary."
—JOHN R. W. STOTT[8]

saying to yourself…" or "You may be thinking, what difference does this make in terms of how I live?" By including questions as part of your message, you assist the receivers by focusing their thoughts and, in many cases, acknowledging the issues they'd raise if you were in a conversation. Sometimes the best messages do not provide answers as much as they ask the right questions.

WHAT BELIEVERS WANT AND NEED

Christian RAP: I'm not advocating a music style. RAP stands for Reticular Activator byPass. God has wired humans with a system called the reticular activator that screens stimuli that are considered harmless and redundant. It might also be called the "been there, done that" button.

Let's say your bathroom mirror cracks. The first week, whenever you look in the mirror, all you see is this unsightly crack. The second week you notice it but get on with your grooming. Two months later, a guest uses the bathroom and comments, "How did your mirror get cracked?" You respond, "Oh, I don't even notice it anymore." You told the truth because your brain has accepted this as a trivial nonevent that shouldn't trigger your attention or consume your energy.

People raised in Christian environments are bombarded with Bible stories, terms, and traditions that tend to get categorized by our reticular activators as unimportant only because we've heard them before. They've become familiar. That's why it's been said the professional ministry is dangerous to our souls because we run the risk of losing the freshness of walking with God due to our immersion in theological work.

Effective communicators understand the challenges of this cranial wiring system. It requires them to create bypass systems so previously heard concepts do not get filtered out by the listeners' RA screens. To do this, you need to use terms and concepts that are less traditional or not likely to have been experienced in the past, or at least not in the same way. Throughout the Sermon on the Mount, Jesus said, "You have heard, but I tell you…" He got people's attention by employing new views of ancient truths. The risk is that some Christians will not consider this Christianity, much the way the Pharisees rejected the teachings of Jesus as heretical. They'd never heard kingdom talk expressed in such a manner. There's often a fine line between getting the attention of sea-soned saints and setting off their heresy detectors. The Christlike method is to do so without compromising the essence of the Scriptures.

WARNING: COMMUNICATING MAY BE HAZARDOUS TO YOUR HEALTH

"Don't be in any rush to become a teacher, my friends. Teaching is highly responsible work. Teachers are held to the strictest standards" (James 3:1, The Message).

Faux Maturity: Most believers want to know more about God and the Bible and how Jesus should influence their lives on a daily basis. Peo-ple tend to be self-centered before they become Christians, and this ori-entation often does not change once they choose to be Christ-followers. That means that they become self-centered Christians who are more inter-ested in having their family members' needs met than they are in reach-ing out to others. Self-centered believers are interested in "what's in it for me." While on one hand we applaud their perceived desire to grow, this is often selfishness dressed in religious garb. They plead for deeper ser-mons, more expository teaching, and churchy programs for their children and teens.

A person I know was interviewing with two large congregations that had contacted him in their search for a pastor. One rejected him because they had no desire to become a seeker-sensitive congregation (using contemporary language for evangelistic purposes), preferring a contem-porary Christian format. The other rejected him because he did not believe in teaching the doctrine of eternal security, a theological hobby horse which to them transcended discussions of personal integrity, pas-sion for the lost, and vision for spiritual maturity. The sad point is that most Christians are more interested in perpetuating their causes than they are in reaching God's lost kids. Behind the mask of righteousness and piety, more often than not, lies a heart of self-centeredness.

Every Jesus-follower deserves the opportunity to take the next step closer to God. But many long-time church attendees need to be lovingly confronted about *faux maturity.* The situation is so common that ministers joke (without laughter) about the parishioner who meets them at the door and says, "Pastor, we've decided to leave the church. We just need more meat."

Never assume that Christians know what they need.

Let's take this moment to address a common myth about "preaching lite." First of all, when people use the *meat* reason, most of them think they are being biblical. But they are taking the concept out of context:

> In fact, though by this time you ought to be teachers, you need someone to teach you the elementary truths of God's word all over again. You need milk, not solid food! Anyone who lives on milk, being still an infant, is not acquainted with the teaching about righteousness. But solid food is for the mature, who by constant use have trained themselves to distinguish good from evil (Hebrews 5:12-14).

The problem described in Hebrews 5 is that the congregants had received sufficient instruction but *their knowledge level far exceeded their obedience quotient.* They failed to apply what they already knew and, thus, failed to mature. The author of Hebrews seems to be implying that maturity is a result of applying the milk—"by constant use have trained themselves."

Being solely a student of the Word will take us only so far. There comes a point in our growth when we must become teachers. As teachers we continue to learn, but a significant part of our maturation comes via investing what we know in others. Those without the gift of group teaching can do this via one-on-one mentoring. Consumeristic believers think that the primary purpose of the pastor is to "feed me, feed me," rather than "equip me, equip me" (Ephesians 4). Self-ascribed spiritual carnivores pile their Bible conference notebooks and sermon outlines on their shelves, taking improper pride in all they've accomplished in their walk with God (James 1:22-25). Like Jack Horner, they pull out their thumbs and say, "What a good boy am I!"

Most of the time, what so-called meat-eaters are suggesting when they leave a church is that they want a certain style of teaching—heavier exposition, word studies, historicity, and biographical background. Some pastors' messages truly are light in biblical content. But more often, popular

American seekers are very open to talking about God and Jesus, as long as it's with an attitude that's open and not pushy and with language they understand.

communication is unfairly criticized for being "content lite" when it is full of very meaty truths. People are often responding to the appearance and not the actual weight of the message. They feel like they get more out of it if you say "sanctification" instead of "spiritual growth."

So how do you create a palatable meal that is also nutritious? When designing a message that seeks to connect with newer believers and seekers, make sure you clearly define what the biblical truth looks like in everyday life at the same time that you help the veteran believer do a self-assessment. When church vets have heard the same concept a few times, they're under the impression that they've applied it. Chances are good that either they haven't or they've become complacent and not taken it to the next level. Most authentically seeker-sensitive messages have enough meat in them to satisfy veteran churchgoers if they seriously devoted themselves to working on the truth that week. Encourage everyone to ask, "How do I know that I've adequately applied this truth in my life?" Then suggest in so many words, "If you know you've applied these things in your life, the next step for your growth is to very intentionally begin teaching others and mentoring them to do the same."

There is a legitimate place for deeper discipleship and stimulating doctrinal education. Limitations of Sunday morning, large-group communication do not allow for this, but seeker-sensitive churches that do not provide for these deeper discussions are derelict. Doctrinal teaching deserves a format in which dialogue can occur, questions can be asked, and specific issues can be unpacked. This requires a classroom or, better yet, a living room setting where learning is enhanced by interaction. Spiritual formation takes place best in a small group where community, accountability, and an emphasis on personal sharing are basic principles.

Most churches and Christians grossly overestimate the ability of a large group worship/teaching service to take believers to the level they need to reach. By providing an array of small groups, you can specifically design levels of discipleship that match the needs of individuals.

HOW TO ADDRESS BOTH GROUPS AT THE SAME TIME

Creative Simplicity

Been there, done that. Heard that, check out. "Tell me something I don't already know," is the pew plea. Regardless of whether you're investigating a unique Bible passage or a well-worn trail, you have to present principles in ways that don't elicit yawns. "God is love. Love other people. Jesus wants to forgive you…blah, blah, blah." These are powerful truths, but if you can't put them into terms that will re-engage the interest and imagination of hearers, they're apt to be lost. Jesus warned about casting pearls before swine. Sometimes rich folk don't appreciate pearls either because they have so many of them or have been around them so long. Although you can get away with stating basic Christian truths for a while when communicating to seekers, you can't do that continually if you hope to connect with mixed audiences—unless you do it with new twists.

Musicians take thirteen basic notes and put them into countless unique arrangements. Authors take twenty-six letters and sell millions of books (not this one). Moviemakers take just a few themes such as tragedy, comedy, and romance and come up with an array of creative combinations. Those who don't, bomb. Even if it's a basic truth, don't say it in a way that's been said a million times before. Let the veteran walk away saying, "I've never heard it that way before. I've not thought of it in that light." A creative approach helps veterans avoid the boredom that comes with familiarity. A simple approach helps seekers who need the basics and get lost in complex themes.

Emphasize Application

As we stated, the typical Christian's Bible knowledge far exceeds his obedience. If you only espouse the truth without focusing on application, veterans of the faith will assume that they already know the information and will be bored. The seeker tends to want application anyway, since he or she is fed up with people who talk Christianity but don't act like Christians. (Many true believers are fed up with them too.) In other words, emphasizing application can engage both believers and seekers. Feel free to take some potshots (generically) at people who profess one thing yet live otherwise. Christians need it, and seekers applaud the emphasis on authenticity. Not only that, but the people who are actually living it admire you for trying to hold others accountable.

There should be something for everyone—even when you're dealing with the basics—if you're talking about living out faith in everyday life. It's a myth that you can't talk about discipleship and nonevangelistic topics when pre-Christians are present. They want to know what faith looks like when it's worn, not just hanging in the store window. For example, don't run away from financial stewardship. Just avoid traditional, guilt-inflicting approaches to the topic. We once had a need to do a mini capital campaign at the same time we were doing a community outreach. The result was a series that looked like this:

How to Get What You Want and Want What You Have

1. "I Can't Get No Satisfaction," But Why?
2. How Much Is Enough?
3. Why Is Money Such a Big Deal? (The Spirituality of Money)
4. What Does God Want From Me Anyway?

In 1954, Kenneth Taylor began translating the New Testament from the King James version to everyday English so his kids could understand it, working on the project during his daily train commute to Chicago. Publishers would not accept this paraphrase, so he self-published what would become *The Living Bible*—which went on to sell more than forty million copies.

"When the time came to name his publishing house, Taylor selected the name of the 16th-century English translator William Tyndale. Tyndale's purpose in translating the Bible was that 'every plowboy could read the Scripture for himself.' "[9]

Filter Language

If you want a message to connect with irreligious people, you need to purge terminology that alienates them unless you immediately define it in ways they understand. Jargon refers to shortcut, insider language. When you use words that others do not understand, you're subtly saying, "We belong. You don't." It's akin to the feeling you have when you're the new boyfriend attending your girlfriend's family event or the husband being dragged to your wife's high school reunion.

When you begin looking for Christian-ese, you realize how often we use words and phrases (without even thinking about it) that don't connect with people who do not have the same background. Below I've listed fifty-five words and phrases that you would do well to either avoid or define. You may want to expand the list, depending on your audience. This is in no way designed to be antibiblical or contra-doctrinal, so please do not consider this heretical. Consider yourself a missionary who must speak a new language to people unaccustomed to our ways. It's been said that you don't really know the definition of a term until you can describe the concept without using the word itself. Harry Beckwith said, "A French mathematician devised the first rule of communicating: 'A theory is not complete until you can explain

saved	sin	blood of Christ	grace (prevenient)
carnal	(entirely) sanctified	holiness	redeemed
regenerate	fellowship	blessing/blessed	hell (fire and brimstone)
heaven	repent	pray through	Holy Spirit
Spirit-filled	rededicate	apostate	born again
washed in the blood	eternal security	original sin	apocalypse
fruit of the Spirit	baptism of the Holy Spirit	washed in the blood of the Lamb	atonement
rapture	white throne judgment	dispensation	tithe
accept Christ	Lord of your life	Holy Trinity	Pentecost(al)
believer	sacrificial giving	stewardship	evangelical
backslidden	Christian/non-Christian	Great Commission	reprobate
spiritual discipline	praise the Lord	hallelujah	anointed
consecrate your heart	the Word (of God)	old nature/new nature	lost
seeker	pagan	nonbeliever	(add your own ideas)

Seek out uncommon ways to say common things...
(Hint: To find uncommon words, try WordNet at cogsci.princeton.edu. Type in a conventional word and WordNet will show you several more interesting ones.)
—HARRY BECKWITH[11]

it to the first person you meet on the street.' "[10] If we're in command of the principles we're teaching, explaining these meanings clearly should not intimidate us.

You can also add anything that is King James– or Elizabethan-sounding, along with denominational terms and acronyms.

Connecting with the churched and unchurched in the same venue is possible if you work hard at conveying the right attitude, focusing on application, and eliminating terms that alienate. Bridging gaps in diverse audiences is a growing need within congregations that hope to connect with spiritual explorers in the twenty-first century.

"After last week's message in Exodus some of you complained that the sermon just didn't touch you. You didn't feel anything..."

PREACH TO REACH

If you have (or develop) the ability to connect with the unchurched, make sure you leverage that. One of the best ways to determine if you have this ability is by surveying newcomer groups to find out why they returned a second, third, and fourth time. When people say, "It's the pastor's speaking," see who's saying it. If it's people who had given up on church or have no church background, chances are you have that ability.

Create message series that grip the interests of the unchurched. Launch these at strategic times (Easter, Christmas Eve, spring, fall, New Year's, and so on) in order to engage people's attention and keep them coming back. Promote these in mail-outs, advertising, and Friend Day fliers. Teach your people to use message series as a tool to invite their friends and neighbors. Don't hide this skill under a basket. Let it shine.

Discussion/Thought Prompters

1. What is your experience in formally communicating with seekers and churched receivers?
2. What are the differences that make this challenging for you?
3. Review a recent message you've given. How would you change it to make it more friendly to seekers?
4. Why is it unlikely that most pastors find out why seekers do not feel comfortable in their churches or listening to them speak?
5. What words or terms would you add or subtract from the list on page 141? How would you define them *without using the term itself?*

Section 2

But Wait, There's More!

The purpose of this book is to provide practical ideas for communicating in the church today. Because our focus is *communication*, there are
vital aspects of preaching untouched, such as homiletics, hermeneutics,
biblical exegesis, and systematic theology. But even as a communication
book, there are a few ministry areas begging to be addressed. The final
three chapters provide application ideas for these: outreach marketing,
writing, and weekly message preparation and presentation.

Chapter Eleven

Market
Well

RETURN TO RENAISSANCE

An ad is a message that makes an impression about your congregation or a ministry event in your church. It is a public message that usually has a cost, so you want to make sure you've designed it to connect. Advertising firms utilize many of the message-design principles in the first ten chapters. Today there are exciting tools for church marketing that including Web sites, DVD business cards, and four-color direct-mail pieces. Now you can bring economical media to your community to let people experience your church without ever leaving their homes.

As our society approaches a twenty-first–century version of the Renaissance, the use of visual arts will play a growing part in communication. Eye-catching pictures, graphics, and icons that represent your church are strong ways to attract would-be attendees. The goal of advertising and marketing is primarily evangelism, not just ego promotion or sheer congregational growth. Today's church leader who wants to embrace the local community needs to be shrewd and savvy in outreach-message creation. As we move toward a post-Christian culture in America, churches cannot rest on drawing only those people already motivated to find a church.

TEN COMMANDMENTS OF CHURCH ADS

1. Thou shalt market. *Marketing* is a modern word for outreach. Some churches grow without any type of advertising, but it's rare. Most of us need advertising to help create some momentum and community awareness.

2. Thou shalt look contemporary. Make sure the appeal is up to date and avoids traditional religious icons. Unless you're intentionally striving for a churched look, do your best to look as contemporary as possible.

3. Thou shalt have all necessary info—a map, address, contact info, Web site, telephone number, dates, times, and whatever else is pertinent. Double-check to make sure the ad has all the important information and that it's correct.

4. Thou shalt not use clichés and jargon. If you want to know how not to do it, look at most church ads around Easter and Christmas or in the church ad section of the newspaper.

5. Thou shalt make it look professional. There's no excuse for shoddy, mediocre ads. Color design and printing are now affordable for even small budgets, so if you're going to market, do it with excellence. Reversed ads stand out best, with white text on a black background. Tall news ads are better than flat or square ones. Four-color, glossy postcards make more sense than one- or two-color letters in envelopes. Keep copy light and graphics bold. The key is image more than content; you can give them the content after you've persuaded them to come.

6. Thou shalt know the audience. Who are you trying to reach: the churched, unchurched, old, young, singles, families? What do they read, buy, and attend? Don't promise something you can't provide. For example, if you want to reach the unchurched, make sure you have a service that really connects with them when they come for a test-drive. Don't pretend to be hip if you're not or contemporary if you're traditional. If your promotion is high quality, make sure the music and nursery match it.

7. Thou shalt use advertising strategically. Promote the events and programs that are most apt to reach people, not the run-of-the-mill functions. If your dollars are limited, start with Easter and Christmas. Then add a fall, spring, and/or New Year outreach focus. If you are marketing to the unchurched, you can advertise in the religious section on Christmas and Easter (cultural religious holidays), but stick to nonchurch sections otherwise (entertainment, sports, lifestyles, and so on).

8. Thou shalt be good stewards. Find out what sort of marketing works best for your area. Community fun days, direct mail, news ads, Web sites, coupon ads, phone book ads, door hangers, billboards/street signs, and radio and TV ads are all vehicles, but usually only two or three will work effectively in a given area. When new people come, make sure you ask them how they found out about your church. Marketing people usually tell you that a rifle is better than a shotgun, targeting a specific group versus saturating a local area. I've not found that to be true. People usually come as a result of multiple sightings rather than a single marketing piece.

9. Thou shalt double-check before going to press and again before mailing. Always assume an ad is incorrect. Have a couple of people look for typos, grammatical errors, or other inaccuracies.

10. Thou shalt not rely solely on advertising. Personal evangelism is always the key to biblical outreach, so don't think you can buy your way into the Great Commission. Advertising helps your people by creating name recognition and familiarity, making it easier for them to invite and more effective when they come.

There is a growing number of organizations that can serve the local

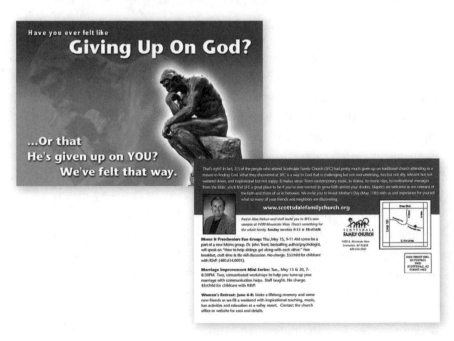

church with contemporary, relevant marketing resources. Here are a few good examples:

Selling the Invisible: A Field Guide to Modern Marketing and *What Clients Love: A Field Guide to Growing Your Business* by Harry Beckwith (Warner Books, Inc.)

Marketing the Church: What They Never Taught You about Church Growth by George Barna (NavPress)

Positioning: The Battle for Your Mind by Al Ries and Jack Trout (McGraw-Hill Trade)

Communication Arts Design Annual

www.outreachmarketing.com

"Of course, when I said 'In conclusion,' I never expected a response like this!"

Chapter Twelve

Write to
Convince

T he power of the pen has evolved into the power of the word processor. Communication is not only a matter of what you say but also how you say it. Sometimes the best way to make your point is in writing. Effective communicators understand when it's best to write rather than speak. Whether it's a letter, note, e-mail, memo, article, or book, writing plays a powerful role in our society today, but it needs to be used wisely. While our emphasis has been on the spoken word, we'd be remiss if we discussed communication without discussing writing.

PROS OF WRITING

• **Writing refines your thinking.** Actually, it doesn't clarify your thinking as much as it helps you realize how muddy your thinking is. We often assume we're doing a better job than we really are when we rely on the spoken word. Writing makes us think through what we're striving to say so we choose just the right words. It's a good way to determine whether we're saying what we mean. If your writing is not clear, then invest more time thinking through what you're really trying to say or accomplish with your message.

"Be careful that you write accurately rather than much."
—Erasmus[1]

• **Writing provides documentation of your message.** It is more difficult for someone to misquote you when your words are in black and white. If you're liable to be misunderstood or if a message is vital, writing is a good medium to reduce hearsay. Make sure you keep hard or digital copies of important correspondence and messages so you can refer to them if people seem confused.

• *Writing provides an echo effect after you're gone.* The written message can be processed whenever it is convenient for the receiver.

• *Writing can cover more bases.* On any given weekend, one-third to two-thirds of your regular attendees are not in a service. If you have an important message to convey, sending it in writing is a way to touch everyone.

The editing professionals at Group Publishing offer you the opportunity to learn secrets that will increase the impact of your ministry writing. For information and dates on their Ministry Writing Summit, see www. grouppublishing .com/summit _experiences.

CONS OF WRITING

• *Writing used to confront can come back to bite you* if you've overstated your case or written the message when you're upset. People tend to soften their words when they're meeting face to face. Always try to avoid confronting people with notes, letters, and e-mails. It's a cowardly approach that can devalue relationships. People deserve the respect of being confronted face to face.

• *Writing can leave a bad impression if you use it poorly.* Improper grammar, typos, inaccurate information, and shabbily constructed sentences lower credibility. When people see something in print, they often give it greater weight, so the message's quality has a great impact on the credibility of the message and its sender—both good and bad.

• *Writing reduces feedback.* You don't know what mood the receivers are in or even who is reading the message. Are they in a good frame of mind or a terrible one? If a person has a question, he'll usually mentally answer it negatively rather than positively. Because he can't ask you what you meant, you may be perceived as saying something that you never intended.

• *Writing can get lost with junk mail and busyness.* Face-to-face, live communication increases the chances that you'll be heard at least once. When you write a letter, e-mail, or newsletter, it will compete with any number of other written messages, increasing its chances of being overlooked.

English Signs Seen in Non-English–Speaking Countries
(Writing well isn't easy.)

- In a Paris hotel elevator: "Please leave your values at the front."
- In a Rome laundry: "Ladies, leave your clothes here and spend the afternoon having a good time."
- In a Norwegian cocktail lounge: "Ladies are requested not to have children in the bar."
- On the menu of a Swiss restaurant: "Our wines leave you nothing to hope for."
- Outside a Hong Kong tailor shop: "Ladies may have a fit upstairs."
- In a Bangkok dry cleaner's: "Drop your trousers here for best results."[2]

DIFFERENCES BETWEEN WRITING AND SPEAKING

More people can speak well than write effectively. That may be hard to believe with so many books on the market, but just because you can formulate thoughts for speaking doesn't mean you can do the same in writing. Many pastors assume they can write a book because they get good feedback from parishioners, but when they begin to write, they discover how different and difficult it can be. Of course, there are also writers who are poor speakers. Writing well requires a different skill set. You cannot merely transcribe your sermons to turn them into manuscripts. Famous pastor/authors usually have professional writers who edit and adapt their transcriptions. Some even have ghostwriters who do a majority of the writing for them. (If you don't like this book, there's no phantom to blame.)

Written communication must rely on word choice to guide the receiver's flow of thought. The spoken word has nonverbal elements such as gestures, vocal modulation, and eye contact. The spoken word tends to be choppier, whereas writing needs to flow. We tend to speak more conversationally and use fillers more often than is acceptable in written form. Most writing should utilize more word pictures, metaphors, and stories because we cannot rely on vocal inflections, nonverbal communication, and speaker energy.

> *"The point of good writing is knowing when to stop."*
> —L.M. MONTGOMERY[3]
>
> *"To write simply is as difficult as to be good."*
> —W. SOMERSET MAUGHAM[4]

FAST RULES FOR EFFECTIVE WRITING

Writing usually requires some talent and a lot of perseverance. Having published ten books prior to this one, I'll never forget an English professor in college who discouraged me by saying, "Alan, you may want to consider a remedial writing course because you're not very good at it." I was disappointed because I always thought I'd be an author. But I was told that I may not have the wiring to ever write effectively. So don't be discouraged if you want to write, but realize that it's not apt to come quickly or easily. The following ideas are not meant to pre-empt a writing course or years of trial and error, but since every pastor needs to write to some extent, here are some basic do's and don'ts.

• Unless you're methodical, find someone who'll proofread for spelling errors. Even detailed-oriented people tend to overlook their own mistakes because they're so familiar with their messages and what they wanted to say.

• Even if you're good at grammar, have someone edit your work for proper punctuation, word choice, and flow. It takes years to learn good writing techniques, so most pastors are better off to find a journalist or English teacher who's adept at grammatical editing. This is different from mere spelling checks.

• If the message is especially important and/or confrontational, make sure you give it a couple of days to cook and then let someone who is mature and knows you look it over for feeling and content. I've learned the hard way that my best efforts are tainted by my own anger, weariness, or degree of awareness. Different perspectives can make the message better, if we're open to their input and advice. It's easier to avoid messes than it is to clean them up.

• Get to the point. Try to confine letters to a single page. Edit your work two to four times to ensure conciseness. Wandering written

"An intellectual is a man who takes more words than necessary to tell more than he knows."

—Dwight D. Eisenhower[5]

messages lose receivers as much as spoken messages do.

• Make it look nice. One of word processing's beauties is that you can easily employ large, readable fonts and quickly rearrange copy so that it's visually attractive. You're competing with professionally designed letters and brochures. Feel free to underline, use bold or italics, and even use color to make your point. All thoughts are not created equal, so be sure to drive your point home.

• Be legal. There's greater accountability in writing than speaking when you quote another person or published work. Make sure you acknowledge other people's ideas as well as words.

• Be positive. Writing, like speaking, should have a residual affect that accomplishes the goal you have in mind. Is the purpose to inform, inspire, persuade, or entertain? What do you want readers to do because of your writing? Ask for the sale. Don't waste their time with unnecessary words. If you write just to write, you'll condition your receivers to toss the really important written messages into the trash with the other junk mail.

> In *Grammatical Man: Information, Entropy, Language, and Life*, Jeremy Campbell addresses the relationship between brevity and clarity. He writes, "In nearly all forms of communication more messages are sent than are strictly necessary to convey the information intended by the sender."
>
> Ironically, he could have cut his sentence in half, and said: "Most people say more than they need to convey their message."
> —Harry Beckwith[6]

Chapter Thirteen

But What About...?

We have covered a lot of ground regarding what causes a message to connect with today's audiences, but what about the nuts and bolts of message preparation? Even veteran preachers like to share stories of what works for them, knowing that we can always improve. Here are a few of the more common topics that arise when pastors talk about the nitty-gritty of their weekly preparation.

1. SHOULD YOU PREACH FROM A MANUSCRIPT OR AN OUTLINE?

Approximately one-fourth of pastors prefer manuscript format because the word-for-word dictation allows them to think through the right terms and poetic flow.[1] Deliberate key phrases and wording are not lost due to memory lapses during the presentation. Those who prefer an outline in various degrees of detail (approximately two-thirds), suggest their way is the best because they are not forced to stay close to their manuscripts.[2] They can better engage the audience with quality eye contact, and they are freer to present a message that connects with receivers.

Whichever way works best for you is fine, but I think working from an outline is the better way if you can do so adequately. A majority of communication is nonverbal (some suggest 70 to 85 percent or more),

> *"The best leaders...almost without exception and at every level, are master users of stories and symbols."*
> —TOM PETERS[3]

so connecting with receivers is greatly enhanced with quality eye contact, animation, and speaker movement. These are limited when you're tied to a manuscript. Good outline speakers give the audience the feeling that they are together, building a relationship. Manuscript readers often have inhibited gestures and vocal range because they are concentrating on their text. Some people get the feeling that they didn't need to attend church to get the gist of the message. They could have gotten the tape or had it e-mailed to them in written form. These may seem like harsh words, but manuscript users need to understand the risks as they try to connect with a twenty-first–century audience. If you use a manuscript, work hard to avoid these downsides.

I suppose the best of both worlds would be manuscript writing for word selection, followed by adequate rehearsal to prevent reliance on the manuscript. Not many have the time or ability to do this, but it affords the strengths of both approaches.

A very small group speaks without any notes, but the potential downsides of wandering, forgetting key points, and repeating oneself tend to make this method less desirable, especially among those of us whose memories are not what they used to be.[4]

2. WHERE DO YOU FIND GOOD ILLUSTRATIONS?

The best illustrations are personal ones. Nothing beats a good story stemming from firsthand experience. When receivers have rapport with a pastor, they are emotionally interested in his or her life. Personal stories are, therefore, more interesting than secondhand ones. A good communicator can create a number of tie-ins to the message with a modest amount of thoughtfulness. A frequent review of current and future preaching topics helps the subconscious come up with a variety of illustrations that would otherwise be forgotten. This is one of the key benefits to planning your message topics. Keep your eyes open while you shop and commute, eavesdrop on coffee shop conversations, and traverse family life issues. Never underestimate the power of unpacking a simple everyday event. At the same time, be cautious about telling personal stories that seem to be unrelated to the point you're trying to make. You don't want to appear to be self-centered or a showoff.

A secondary illustration source is stories you may find from others, by reading the paper or a news magazine or scanning the Internet. These tend to be more current and are less likely to have been used in the past. Referring to current events shows that you are engaged in everyday matters. Citing trends, statistics, and data is a good way to engage logic-oriented receivers.

The very last resort is to rely on illustrations from books and some pastoral Web sites. These canned approaches to sermon illustrations usually fall flat when you incorporate them into a message. Avoid old church jokes, stories, and clichés. These tend to work against you when people hear you say things that many have heard a dozen times. If you want to repeat even a good story within a year or two, you'll want to precede it with a disclaimer such as, "One of my favorite stories is..." or "I've told this before, but..." That way you acknowledge that some people are thinking, "There he goes again; I've heard this one before." (Of course, if you change pastorates every three or four years, there's little chance of repeating stories to the same audience anyway.)

The best way to discover statistical data on specific topics is to do an Internet search. Since Web addresses keep changing, I hesitate to list any here, but a great information site provided by the U.S. census is factfinder.census.gov.

No matter what stories you tell, creative use of visual aids has a lingering affect. If you're mentioning 1 Corinthians 14:8 on the "uncertain sound of a trumpet," hold up a horn. If you're discussing Jesus' talk about blind people leading blind people (Matthew 15:14), enter with dark sunglasses and a white cane. Video media, computer graphics, large platform displays, visual aids, and audience participation are all effective means of illustrating a point. Consider using other people as visual aids, letting them tell their stories on video, live, or via an interview. As a rule of thumb, plan for two to four illustrations per info chunk.

3. IS IT OK TO PREACH SOMEONE ELSE'S MATERIAL? HOW FAR SHOULD YOU GO IN REFERENCING?

Ah, the age-old question of being original and boring or creative and a thief. While lawyers and legalists may disagree with me, my rule of thumb is as follows:

If you're using someone else's message outline, make sure you record it in your notes, but you don't need to admit that it came from someone else unless your messages are going to be broadcast or published beyond local use. The fact that you've referenced it in your notes denotes your admission that it originated somewhere else. If someone asks for the source, you can provide it. Obviously, extended word-for-word use would not be appropriate.

If you quote from a book or magazine, you should cite the reference verbally. Doing so can actually add credibility, as long as it is not a long quote that begins to bore people. But you don't want to bog down your message with too many reference citations and disclaimers.

If you are publishing or broadcasting your message, then accountability takes on a new level. Most copyright holders allow fifty to five hundred words to be used without permission, but unless you know who permits what amount, you'll need to check with the specific publisher. Most have phone numbers or e-mail addresses on their Web sites specifically for permission requests. Song lyrics and poems are another matter. These usually require written permission to use. Plan on paying a royalty fee. An exception would be Christian songs covered under your CCLI license (www.ccli.com).

Honesty in research and being fair to originators are both legal and moral issues that should not be taken lightly. I remember someone giving me a book on a topic similar to one of my books. As I perused the book, I read a passage that was almost word for word from my book but without any reference. When I wrote the author, he apologized, admitting he'd lost the reference. If you publish or broadcast your work, it's your responsibility to keep records of the research if you want to use it.

4. WHAT'S BETTER: TOPICAL OR EXPOSITORY PREACHING?

We touched on this briefly in the opening chapters. Topical preaching usually begins with the audience's interests and felt needs. What does the Bible say about marriage, work, challenges, failure, and family? This is where most of our people live on a regular basis, and these messages tend to connect well. But relying too much on topical preaching can give receivers a piecemeal feel for the Scriptures. We lift out texts that illustrate specific points but rarely get to know characters, doctrines, and book themes within the Bible in much detail. My preference is to alternate *biblical* topical with *relevant* expository; the former series addresses a felt need, and the latter begins with a specific book or passage.

"We are drowning in information but starved for knowledge."
—JOHN NAISBITT[5]

Expository preaching allows the Scripture to set the agenda for our preaching. A book or biographical series lets the Bible speak for itself. Our job is primarily to unpack what exists in the Bible rather than creating a structure that fits our felt needs. But merely exposing Scripture is insufficient; that's teaching, not preaching. We need to reveal the relevance of the passage. Good missionaries can translate meaning from one language to another. Missional communicators connect ageless Bible truths with the culture of the day so that people can understand and apply it. Alternating topical and expository series seems to provide the best of both worlds.

Some people who label themselves as Bible expositors are really topical preachers in disguise. Instead of looking at a passage with a magnifying glass, they use a microscope. They take each individual word or phrase and turn it into its own topical study. That gives the impression that you're getting an intimate look at Scripture, but in reality you're losing the essence of its true meaning. If you analyze any paragraph of this book on a word-by-word basis, you're apt to miss its true meaning. Meaning is gained when you understand how the words affect each other in the context of the entire work. Effective expositors strive to uncover the contextual meaning of a passage and then relate it to everyday terms. Microanalyzing a passage causes people to lose understanding.

While inductive preaching implies beginning with the text for deeper exposition, and deductive preaching suggests starting with a question begging to be answered, a hard separation of the two ideas is just convenient fiction for theological classroom discussions. It's possible to craft an inductive topical message and a deductive expository message. Too much of either one in most congregations will result in a communication disconnection.

In today's culture, three- to twelve-week miniseries work well. That lets you develop graphics, promotional materials, and a train of thought that engages people. When you spend six months in the book of Romans, you're running the risk of losing people who are not wired for that close a look at a single book. If you skip around to a different topic each week, there's little for your listeners to anticipate, and you're apt to waste a lot of time contemplating each week's theme. Regular attendees used to average three-plus weeks per month. But now, people consider themselves to be active if they attend only one or two services per month. At that rate, any one person is apt to hear less than half of a series anyway. Topical or expository miniseries allow you to re-engage people who feel they've missed out or are disinterested in a certain theme.

> Since the world in all its fancy wisdom never had a clue when it came to knowing God, God in his wisdom took delight in using what the world considered dumb—*preaching*, of all things!—to bring those who trust him into the way of salvation (1 Corinthians 1:21, *The Message*).

5. HOW MUCH TIME SHOULD YOU PUT INTO WEEKLY MESSAGE PREPARATION?

Everyone is different. Involvement in ministry teams, counseling, pastoral care, and any number of other responsibilities prevent the typical pastor from investing a large amount of time in message preparation. Pastors of larger churches have staff who oversee congregational care and ministries, so there is more time to invest in concentrated study.

A few of my friends who pastor large congregations take two to four weeks of annual study leave, in which they write months of message outlines in concentrated chunks of time. The typical pastor invests six to fifteen hours per week in message prep, from study to organization to writing and rehearsing. Weekly prep takes longer when you're starting a new series and doing background research and outlining.

Most of us want more thorough preparation than this, but few of us believe we can justify it in light of our other obligations. The seminary guideline of "one hour prep per one minute in the pulpit" doesn't work for anyone I know. If you consistently take longer than fifteen hours per week in message preparation, you may want to see what you can do to better organize your preparation. You can employ the help of others for research and gathering illustrations, current events, and statistics. As we all know, some messages just seem to flow quickly, whereas others have to be

> *"Make thyself a craftsman in speech, for thereby thou shalt gain the upper hand."*
> —EGYPTIAN TOMB INSCRIPTION[6]

chipped out of stone. Consistently less than six hours may be a sign that you're winging it with shallow content and poorly planned structure. Perhaps you can do this because you're a gifted presenter. But you can't rush quality message crafting. Your heart and subconscious need time to percolate what your conscious is fed.

Knowing where you're headed beforehand can save a lot of time and energy. Planning six to nine months in advance allows you to begin collecting illustrations, stories, articles, and background info, as well as asking others to do the same for you. The benefit of reviewing future message themes every couple of weeks is that you program your subconscious to be on the prowl for materials. Ideas will come to you "out of the blue" which can be recorded, filed, and incorporated during your design time. Sometimes we waste creative time when we only work on a message the week before. It's tough to force creativity. Give your mind time to cook an idea and see how it flows.

Rehearsing a message seems to be a personal matter. Most of us agree it's not much fun. Some preach aloud from the platform a couple of times prior to the service. Others go over their messages out loud in the office. Some just mentally review their notes. Regardless of your preference, it's usually best to fully rehearse introductions, conclusions, and key illustrations. These are too important to be delivered unrehearsed.

6. HOW CAN YOU PUT MORE CREATIVITY INTO YOUR MESSAGES AND SERVICES?

People are hungry for good communication. You'll probably be surprised at how receptive they are to creative ideas that make sense and help them "get" a concept. Knowing your own congregation, you'll need to expand their boundaries judiciously, adding elements here and there as you gradually open the window of acceptance. While some congregations war over musical styles, drama, and even video clips, most will grant the pastor a lot of latitude when it comes to creativity in his speaking.

Church-transformation issues are hot topics these days. (For example, see *How to Change Your Church (Without Killing It)*, Alan Nelson and Gene Appel, W Publishing Group, 2000.) Your foundational calling is to effectively communicate the truths of Christ. That may require the use of nontraditional means in order to reach contemporary audiences. Pick your battles well, but don't hesitate to take on a challenge that can harvest fruit. Most people are fearful of the unknown. But once they experience a new idea and it becomes "known," they're far more accepting. This means you may need to take some risks with creative communication elements. Once you've established the purpose, message tie-in, and biblical support of visual arts, most people will like what they see. When we fail to make the connection and add creativity for creativity's sake, we open ourselves up to legitimate criticism. Start mild and then expand the boundaries, little by little.

If you find that you need to increase the energy of your messages and services by adding creative communication elements, you may want to add a creative team ministry to your preparation. Many churches use creative teams that meet regularly to brainstorm ideas for the service and message, such as video clips, dramas, visual aids, music, special effects, and graphics. We e-mail an outline to our creative team a week or two before our monthly meeting (which is held at night because we have several laypeople). The best team size seems to be four to seven. Things get bogged down with eight or more. You'll want to hand-select creative types who understand the basic goals of your ministry and who seem to come up with consistently good ideas. Some idea people derail a team because they aren't good at seeing the big picture or have personalities that push ideas when they need to rest. Don't forget one or two technical people to help plan the multimedia aspects.

Here's a recent creative team update letter to give you an idea of how one church does it.

SFC CREATIVE TEAM

We wanna be more creative than ever; having fun, being true to the biblical principles, but in ways that make you go "hmm-mmm." As we continue to hone our creative skills, here are some ideas we wanna see implemented this coming year:

1. Our goal is four to six people at Creative Team meetings, but we need at least one person from each of the worship arts departments (band, AV, drama, vocal) with this caveat: COME PREPARED! This means musicians need to have reviewed the outlines and have some songs (secular/Christian) in mind. Cold turkey creativity wastes a lot of time and energy, so prep one to three weeks in advance, make notes, and come ready to share (without assuming your ideas will be implemented, of course). Let your subconscious do the work for you. (See attached message themes.)

2. Even though I'm planning themes four to six months in advance, we'll primarily focus on the next month, giving us a four- to six-week lead.

3. Having said that, we'll try to keep message topics way in front and macro theme art/graphic/illustration ideas on the horizon within our monthly brainstorms. Micro ideas should apply to the next month's worth of message themes, so we can polish as we go, assign responsibilities, and even prep service outlines.

If everyone on the worship team helps by doing some movie/graphic/Web site/music/drama reviews in advance and sending ideas to each other, our time together will be much better spent and absences won't mean we lost your input completely. We'll strive to keep meetings at the church, second Tuesday evening, 7-9:30 p.m. Thanks for making SFC a fun place to seriously worship.

CREATIVE TEAM FORM
Series: Managing the Ups and Downs of Life
> **Theme:** A look at the life of David and his ups and downs, relating to our own highs and lows in life and what we can learn from David's example.
>> Sept. 7: Faith (facing your giants)
>>
>> Sept. 14: Success (handling good times)
>>
>> Sept. 21: Setbacks (encountering enemies)
>>
>> Sept. 28: Failure (making bad decisions)
>>
>> Oct. 5: Worship (experiencing God)
>>
>> Oct. 12: Betrayal (let down by loved ones)
>>
>> Oct. 19: Legacy (ending well)

> **Audio/visual team:** Roller coaster theme, thirty-second intro, starting with click-click sound of coaster car going up the hill, followed by screams and going down first couple of hills. Play this during first three to four weeks of series.
> **Visual aid:** Banners at front of auditorium in monochrome outline of bust of David, plus foam-board-mounted posters in lobby.

Sept. 7: Faith

David and Faith (Goliath) *1 Samuel 17*

Message Goal: *Inspire people to face their giants with renewed confidence, based on faith in God.*

Message Overview: *Faith is a part of our character development, trusting God in facing giants. Consider rewards as well. Classic story of looking at size of God versus circumstances. How do we live by faith like that?*

> **Song/Music:**
>
> **Drama:**
>
> **Movie clip:**
>
> **Visual aid:**
>
> **Miscellaneous:**

Here are some Web sites with great church graphics and resources available as this is being published. Some of these may become dated, but they'll give you an idea of what to look for in terms of effective communication media and graphics:

> *"Communication is the art of being understood."*
> —PETER USTINOV[7]

www.wiredchurches.com

www.fellowshipchurch.com

www.preachingplus.com

www.ginghamsburg.org

www.flagshipchurches.com

In addition, two good resources from Group Publishing are *Designing Worship* and *Holy Wow*.

7. HOW CAN YOU SHARPEN YOUR PRESENTATION SKILLS?

In addition to implementing some of the feedback ideas in Chapter 9, you can take proactive steps toward improving your communication. The best single place I know to spruce up your speaking skills is Toastmasters (www.toastmasters.com). You'll probably find it to be one of the most accepting "churches" you've attended because people are friendly, affirming, and constructive in their suggestions. Most cities have several of these clubs, designed to help members improve their communication skills. Other options are public speaking classes at a local college, university, seminary and a communication coach who can provide mentoring. Most of us would do well to increase the amount of rehearsal time we put into our messages. This can be a torturous process, so we're tempted to skate past it because we know we can "get by." Since most of us consider preaching our primary ministry, whatever we can do to improve our speaking skills will increase our overall effectiveness and fulfillment.

"It's the pastor. He won't jump...It's just his way of dealing with post-sermon depression."

Epilogue

I n spite of technological advancements and extreme cultural shifts, the pastoral proclamation of God's Word is still the backbone of Christian growth and church life. While so many things are changing around us, oral and written communication continues to be the primary way of helping people come to know God. Therefore, the burden is heavy for us to be the best we can be in delivering that life-changing message. Continually sharpening the ax is not optional. Today people are bombarded with a legion of well-crafted messages, designed to divert their attention from the kingdom. We must be shrewd as serpents and harmless as doves as we persuade them to listen to us as we represent their Creator.

Communication is the process of getting a point from one mind to another. Even when that is adequately done, people can always reject it. Make sure you don't confuse a message that is not acted upon with one that does not connect. It's fair to assume that Jesus had the ultimate skill of communicating, yet some of his best efforts were disregarded:

> When you enter a town and are welcomed, eat what is set before you. Heal the sick who are there and tell them, "The kingdom of God is near you." But when you enter a town and are not welcomed, go into its streets and say, "Even the dust of your town that sticks to our feet we wipe off against you. Yet be sure of this: The kingdom of God is near." I tell you, it will be more bearable on that day for Sodom than for that town.
>
> "Woe to you, Korazin! Woe to you, Bethsaida! For if the miracles that were performed in you had been performed in Tyre and Sidon, they would have repented long ago, sitting in sackcloth and ashes" (Luke 10:8-13).

Until you've exhausted the efforts of effective message design, you shouldn't conclude that people are authentically rejecting your content. But if you have truly done all you can, wipe the dust from your sandals and move on down the road. No use in casting pearls before swine, unless of course God has called you to a specific pigpen (Matthew 7:6). Beating yourself up with discouragement or guilt won't help you be more effective in these situations.

I want to end with a prayer for you that is a heartfelt message of hope and blessing on your commitment to improve your communication, whether you're a rookie or a veteran. The craft of communicating to connect is a lifelong process, a destination at which one never truly arrives. Every setting and audience creates new demands that challenge even the most gifted communicator. I hope these ideas have been helpful as you strive to serve God with your abilities and calling.

> *God, bless my friend who has traveled through these pages with a desire to be more effective as a person called by you to communicate the transformational truths of your Word. I pray that this reader will experience a new sense of commitment and a new level of excellence as he or she strives to apply what you've shown in the previous chapters. Your Word is far too precious to be mishandled. You deserve our best presentation. Anoint my fellow communicators as they work at designing messages that connect. Amen.*

Feel free to contact the author at www.leadingideas.org.

OLD PASTORS HOME

PORKOK

Used by artist's permission. Reprinted from Leadership Journal.

Endnotes

INTRODUCTION

1. Patrick O. Marsh, Ph.D., *Messages That Work* (Englewood Cliffs, NJ: Educational Technology Publications, Inc., 1983).

CHAPTER 1

1. Barna Research Online, www.barna.org/cgi-bin/PagePress Release.asp?Press ReleaseID=158&Reference=A.
2. Mark Galli and Craig Brian Larson, *Preaching That Connects: Using the Techniques of Journalists to Add Impact to Your Sermons* (Grand Rapids, MI: Zondervan, 1994), 9.
3. Harry Beckwith, *Selling the Invisible: A Field Guide to Modern Marketing* (New York, NY: Warner Books, Inc., 1997), 170.
4. William Bridges, *Managing Transitions: Making the Most of Change* (New York, NY: Perseus Books, 1991), 15.
5. Anaïs Nin as quoted by Rick Warren in *The Purpose-Driven Life: What on Earth Am I Here For?* (Grand Rapids, MI: Zondervan, 2002), 41.
6. R.C. Sproul, "The Object of Contemporary Relevance," *Power Religion* (Chicago: Moody, 1992), 319.
7. John R. W. Stott, *Between Two Worlds: The Art of Preaching in the Twentieth Century* (Grand Rapids, MI: Wm. B. Eerdmans Publishing Co., 1982), 138-139.
8. University of Phoenix Web site, www.universityofphoenix.com.
9. Haddon W. Robinson, *Preaching* (Grand Rapids, MI: Baker Book House, 1980), 163.
10. Anne Morrow Lindbergh, *Gift From the Sea* (New York, NY: Pantheon Books, 1955), 102.
11. Graham MacPherson Johnston, *Preaching to a Postmodern World: A Guide to Reaching Twenty-First Century Listeners* (Grand Rapids, MI: Baker Books, 2001), 59.
12. Harry Beckwith, *What Clients Love: A Field Guide to Growing Your Business* (New York, NY: Warner Books, Inc., 2003), 76.

CHAPTER 2

1. Galli and Larson, *Preaching That Connects*, 16.
2. As quoted in Johnston, *Preaching to a Postmodern World*, 149.
3. Leslie Parrott, personal interview, Phoenix, AZ, January 18, 2004.
4. As quoted in Johnston, *Preaching to a Postmodern World*, 7.
5. Galli and Larson, *Preaching That Connects*, 19.
6. Marsh, *Messages That Work*, 54.

CHAPTER 3

1. *The Living Webster Encyclopedic Dictionary of the English Language*, 220.
2. Time, Sept. 12, 1960. See www.bartleby.com/63/83/5583.html.
3. Gordon S. Jackson, *Never Scratch a Tiger with a Short Stick and Other Quotations for Leaders* (Colorado Springs, CO: NavPress, 2003), 44.
4. Beckwith, *What Clients Love*, 101.
5. Beckwith, *Selling the Invisible*, 182.

CHAPTER 4

1. Beckwith, *What Clients Love*, 180.
2. Marsh, *Messages That Work*, 64.
3. Ibid., 65.
4. Ibid., xix.

CHAPTER 5

1. Rick Warren, "Put Application Into Your Messages," Rev. (November/December 2003), 24.

CHAPTER 6

1. Robinson, *Preaching*, 160.
2. Beckwith, *Selling the Invisible*, 95.
3. Galli and Larson, *Preaching That Connects*, 36.
4. Beckwith, *What Clients Love*, 259.
5. Stephen R. Covey, *The Seven Habits of Highly Effective People* (New York, NY: Fireside, 1989).
6. Robinson, *Preaching*, 167.
7. Jim Cymbala, *Fresh Power: Experiencing the Vast Resources of the Spirit of God* (Grand Rapids, MI: Zondervan Publishing House, 2001), 55.
8. E.M. Bounds, *Powerful and Prayerful Pulpits* (Grand Rapids, MI: Baker, 1993), 43, as quoted by Cymbala in *Fresh Power*, 58.

CHAPTER 7

1. Lyle Schaller, "Every Part Is an 'I,' " Leadership Journal (Fall 1999), 30.
2. Walter Onn as quoted by Thomas Long, "Preaching With Ordered Passion," Leadership Journal (Spring 1991), 139.
3. Beckwith, *What Clients Love*, 77.
4. William Zinsser, *Writing to Learn*, as quoted by Beckwith in *What Clients Love*, 77.

CHAPTER 8

1. Robinson, *Preaching*, 167.
2. George Edgar Sweazey, *Preaching the Good News* (Englewood Cliffs, NJ: Prentice-Hall, Inc., 1976), 100.
3. Suzette Elgin as quoted in Jackson, *Never Scratch a Tiger with a Short Stick*, 42.
4. Anton Chekhov as quoted in Jackson, *Never Scratch a Tiger with a Short Stick*, 41.

CHAPTER 10

1. Stott, *Between Two Worlds*, 138.
2. *Luther*, screenplay written by Camille Thomasson and Bart Gavigan, Copyright: NFP teleart 2003.
3. Phillip Yancey live lecture, San Diego, CA: September 30, 2003.
4. Beckwith, *Selling the Invisible*, 99.
5. Beckwith, *What Clients Love*, 101.
6. Johnston, *Preaching to a Postmodern World*, 78.
7. Ibid., 88-89.
8. Stott, *Between Two Worlds*, 140.
9. Story of Tyndale publishing from Web site: www.tyndale.com
10. Beckwith, *What Clients Love*, 92.
11. Ibid., 138.

CHAPTER 12

1. Erasmus as quoted in Jackson, *Never Scratch a Tiger with a Short Stick*, 42.
2. Lowell D. Streiker, *Nelson's Big Book of Laughter* (Nashville, TN: Thomas Nelson, Inc., 2000), 86.
3. L.M. Montgomery as quoted in Jackson, *Never Scratch a Tiger with a Short Stick*, 43.
4. W. Somerset Maugham as quoted in Jackson, *Never Scratch a Tiger with a Short Stick*, 43.
5. Dwight D. Eisenhower as quoted in Jackson, *Never Scratch a Tiger with a Short Stick*, 42.
6. John Naisbitt as quoted in Beckwith, *What Clients Love*, 76.

CHAPTER 13

1. Leadership Survey, March 1999, published in Leadership Journal (Winter 2000), 49.
2. Ibid.
3. Jackson, *Never Scratch a Tiger with a Short Stick*, 44.
4. Leadership Survey, March 1999, published in Leadership Journal (Winter 2000), 49.
5. Ibid., 43.
6. Ibid., 42.
7. Peter Ustinov as quoted in Jackson, *Never Scratch a Tiger with a Short Stick*, 44.

Appendix A

MESSAGE CONNECTIVITY ASSESSMENT (MCA)

Thirty questions based on nine of the ten secrets

Please circle your response: 1 not at all, 2 some, 3 moderately, 4 quite a bit, 5 strongly

Secret #1: *Answer the Question "Why Should I Listen to You?"*
1. Did this message quickly convince you that you should listen?
    1 2 3 4 5
2. Was the relevance of the message made clear at the beginning?
    1 2 3 4 5
3. Do you feel that the theme is something you can use in your life?
    1 2 3 4 5

Secret #2: *Know Your Audience*
4. Did the speaker seem to relate to you?
    1 2 3 4 5
5. Did the speaker seem to relate to other people in the audience?
    1 2 3 4 5
6. Did the audience seem to relate to the speaker?
    1 2 3 4 5

Secret #3: *Clarify the Context*
7. Did the message seem to fit the setting in which it was given?
    1 2 3 4 5
8. Was the room free from distractions?
    1 2 3 4 5
9. Were you physically and emotionally comfortable in the setting?
    1 2 3 4 5

Secret #4: *Strategize the Four Primary Message-Design Components*
10. Was the message about the right weight (not too light or too heavy)?
    1 2 3 4 5
11. Was the right amount of new and interesting material presented?
    1 2 3 4 5
12. Was the length of the message right?
    1 2 3 4 5

Secret #5: *Give Them Handles*
13. Do you feel you could apply at least part of today's message?
    1 2 3 4 5
14. Did you receive practical ways to apply the message in your life?
    1 2 3 4 5
15. Did the illustrations and visual aids help you understand the message?
    1 2 3 4 5

Secret #6: *Bait the Hook*
16. Did the opening part of the message grab you?
1   2   3   4   5
17. Did the introduction make you want to listen to the rest of the message?
1   2   3   4   5
18. Did the first part of the message make it clear where we were headed?
1   2   3   4   5

Secret #7: *Avoid the Bore-Snore Factor*
19. Did the message keep your attention?
1   2   3   4   5
20. Did the speaker seem believable and passionate about the theme?
1   2   3   4   5
21. Did the speaker seem anointed, spiritually prepared for the presentation?
1   2   3   4   5

Secret #8: *Ask for the Sale*
22. Were you moved to respond to the message today?
1   2   3   4   5
23. Were you given some sort of response option?
1   2   3   4   5
24. Was it clear how you could implement or apply today's message?
1   2   3   4   5

Secret #9: *Measure Results* (This MCA is the measurement tool.)

Secret #10: *Bridge for Broader Impact*
25. Did the message today connect with most of the people receiving it?
1   2   3   4   5
26. Did the terms and wording make sense?
1   2   3   4   5
27. Would it connect both with people new to Christianity and those familiar with it?
1   2   3   4   5

Summary:
28. Did the speaker connect with his or her audience overall?
1   2   3   4   5
29. Did the ending make sense and conclude the message well?
1   2   3   4   5
30. Do you feel like you got a lot out of today's message?
1   2   3   4   5

You can average each principle, 0 to 15 possible points.

0-5: Message needs significant attention, major threat of disconnect

6-10: Message needs some attention, minor disconnect is possible

11-15: Message is strong; keep polishing rough spots

(You can download a copy of this form without the ten secrets listed in the text from www.leadingideas.org.)

Appendix B

WORKSHEET FOR DETERMINING MESSAGE LOAD

Although communication is more art than science, there are ways to quantifiably estimate whether a message stands a reasonable chance of connecting. Researchers suggest that anything real should be measurable. We've discussed info chunks, density, complexity, audience sophistication, and time in terms of message design. Following is a formula that can help you predict an appropriate message load. It should be helpful in uncovering weaknesses in your message creation. While it's subjective, the mathematical estimates are realistic in terms of what effective communicators do intuitively in developing a message. You may want to let others help you assess the reliability of your estimates in order to improve the connectivity of your messages. This is designed for the typical weekend worship service message or comparable format.

The Info Load formula is:

$$\frac{\text{Info Chunks Index} \times \text{Density/Complexity Index}}{\text{Time Index} \times \text{Sophistication Index}} = \text{Message Load}$$

(Info Churnks Index times Density/Complexity Index, divided by Time Index times Sophistication Index equals Message Load)

Info chunks: Based on the 5±2 principle, choose the appropriate index (1-5) that corresponds to the number of info chunks in your message.

1—1-2 chunks
2—3-4 chunks
3—5-6 chunks
4—7-8 chunks
5—9+ chunks

Density/complexity: This has to do with the simplicity of the message. How much does it tax the brain and senses? Choose the appropriate numerical factor.

1—Very low density: straightforward, singular medium

2—Low density: low key and simple

3—Moderate density: somewhat engaging and stimulating

4—Moderately high density: concentrated, mediated, and stimulating

5—High density: very concentrated, complex, requires engagement

Time: Based on a typical devotional/homily/sermon/seminar setting, the times have been broken down into five categories, allowing you to select the appropriate factor.

1—less than 10 minutes

2—10-20 minutes

3—20-40 minutes

4—40-60 minutes

5—more than 1 hour

Sophistication: This has to do with the receiver's ability to process the message content. Obscurity relates to the message, sophistication to the audience. A sophisticated audience has a low obscurity factor, meaning it is familiar with the content and can process it well.

1—low sophistication (high obscurity): children listening to an adult message

2—modest sophistication (medium-high obscurity): young teens listening to an adult message

3—moderate sophistication (medium obscurity): new believers listening to a message

4—high sophistication (medium-low obscurity): established Christian hearing a sermon

5—very high sophistication (low obscurity): pastor listening to a message

Based on a simple mathematical range, the lowest possible total of these factors would be 0.5 and the highest score would be 25.

Message Load

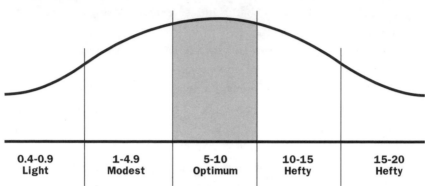

| 0.4-0.9
Light | 1-4.9
Modest | 5-10
Optimum | 10-15
Hefty | 15-20
Hefty |

Depth of development is a direct result of how much time you have and the amount of info chunks. Messages with more info chunks and density over less time could not be developed as deeply as longer messages. For example, you could teach a group of teens some relatively complicated principles if you had plenty of time and could explain, illustrate, and invest energy into each individual point by elaborating it. When your time is reduced, all you can do is skim the topic, providing a shallower message. If you want to put a message load into the optimum range, you'll likely need to increase time or decrease the amount of info chunks you're trying to communicate. Trying to say too much in too little time is poor stewardship, as is saying too little in a long period. Appropriateness and balance are the keys.